Published in 2012 by Stewart, Tabori & Chang
An imprint of ABRAMS

Library of Congress Cataloging-in-Publication Data
Gaughan, Norah.
Comfort knitting & crochet : babies & toddlers : more than 50 knit and crochet
designs using Berroco's comfort and vintage yarns / by Norah Gaughan and the
Berroco Design Team.
    pages cm
ISBN 978-1-58479-987-0
1. Knitting—Patterns. 2. Crocheting—Patterns. 3. Children's clothing. 4. Infants'
clothing. I. Title. II. Title: Babies & toddlers : more than 50 knit and crochet designs
using Berroco's comfort and vintage yarns. III. Title: Comfort knitting and crochet.
  TT825.G2834 2012
  746.434--dc23   2011053262

Editor: Liana Allday
Designer: Onethread Design, Inc.
Production Manager: Tina Cameron

The text of this book was composed in News 702 BT,
Archer, and Avenir.
Printed and bound in the United States

10 9 8 7 6 5 4 3 2 1

115 West 18th Street
New York, NY 10011
www.abramsbooks.com

www.berroco.com
info@berroco.com

COMFORT KNITTING & CROCHET

Babies & Toddlers

50 knit and crochet designs using
Berroco's Comfort and Vintage yarns

Norah Gaughan and the Berroco Design Team

Photographs by Ericka McConnell
Photostyling by Danielle Gold

STC CRAFT | A MELANIE FALICK BOOK
STEWART, TABORI & CHANG
NEW YORK

CONTENTS

knit

crochet

INTRODUCTION
something
for every baby
and toddler

Nothing is quite as exciting as celebrating the arrival of a new baby. And on this happiest of occasions, nothing expresses our love and welcomes the wee recipient as nicely as handmade gifts. In addition to being loving gestures made with our very own hands, baby items are delightfully fun to make. Since baby garments and toys are small, they provide the perfect opportunity to try out new techniques and see fast results. Blankets, of course, require a larger investment of time and yarn, but the effort is well worth it, since blankets tend to become treasured items, used for years to come.

In this book you will find 50 knitted and crocheted items for babies and toddlers, each made with several different weights of the affordably priced Berroco Comfort and Berroco Vintage yarns. Comfort is an ultra-soft blend of super fine acrylic and nylon, spun into a luxury twist usually reserved for the finest merino wools. It is hypoallergenic, can be machine-washed and -dried, and is available in an exquisite range of more than 95 shades. For those who love the qualities wool has to offer but need an easy-to-wash blend, Vintage yarn is a perfect choice. Available in a wide color range, including many irresistible heather shades, it is a blend of wool, acrylic, and nylon, with an incredibly soft touch and yardage that goes on and on.

When we began to design the items for this book, we thought about the variety of approaches people take when dressing young children. Traditionalists, of course, insist on pastels and shades of white, while many modern parents love dressing their babies in brights. Still others prefer a more subdued palette, incorporating browns and grays into baby's wardrobe. Beyond these personal preferences, we tried to consider various climates, and we sought inspiration from several sources, including historical art movements, decorative arts, folk crafts, and our natural surroundings. For instance, the High Fidoodlity (page 49), Moderne (page 67), and Scribble (page 149) blankets were all inspired by midcentury modern art and design, while the inspiration for the Darla (page 17), Rag Rug (page 76), and Butterfly (page 109) blankets began with Depression-era quilts from the 1930s, which were typically fashioned from recycled textiles. Delicately embellished Victorian-era teacups inspired the Limoges Blanket (page 117) and

Sunday Best Dress (page 123), while Mother Nature herself had the most direct influence on our citrus-themed offerings: Key Lime Blanket (page 12), Orangelo Bib (page 15), Pomelo Slice (page 47), Yuzu Blanket (page 89), and Limonia Caterpillar (page 146). And of course, we couldn't resist taking inspiration from our own lives and family histories. The Slice Cap and the Hike Hat (on pages 28 and 134) were inspired by the black-and-white photo at left, which features my friend Cynthia's father, Russ Sherwin, and his buddies in early 1940s Wyoming.

The projects in *Comfort Knitting & Crochet: Babies & Toddlers* are intended for every skill level, from beginner to advanced. We hope that you will turn to it for baby and toddler projects for many years to come.

Cleire
Cardigan

Crocheted bobbles and diamond cables come together to make this sweet, feminine cardigan. The yoke, front panels, and all the edges are defined by the bobbles, which are inspired by the pebble beaches on Ireland's southernmost inhabited island, Cleire.

SIZES
3 (6, 9, 12, 18, 24) months

FINISHED MEASUREMENTS
18 (19¼, 20, 22, 24, 26)" chest

YARN
Berroco Comfort DK (50% super fine nylon / 50% super fine acrylic; 50 grams / 178 yards): 3 (3, 3, 3, 4, 4) skeins
#2703 Barley

CROCHET HOOKS
Crochet hook size US H/8 (5 mm)
Change hook size if necessary to obtain correct gauge.

NOTIONS
Stitch markers; two ½" buttons

GAUGE
20 sts and 20 rows = 4" (10 cm) in Single Crochet (sc)

ABBREVIATIONS
FPdc: Yo, insert hook from front to back to front around post of indicated st, yo and pull up a loop, [yo and pull through 2 loops on hook] twice.
FPdc decrease: Yo, insert hook from front to back to front around post of first skipped FPdc, yo and pull up a loop, yo and draw through 2 loops on hook; yo, insert hook from front to back to front around post of next skipped FPdc, yo and pull up a loop, yo and draw through 2 loops on hook, yo and draw through all 3 loops on hook.

Popcorn: Work 5 sc in next sc, drop loop from hook, insert hook in first sc of this 5-sc group then through dropped loop, draw dropped loop through st. Ch 1 to close (ch does not count as a st).
Sc2tog: Pull up a loop in each of next 2 sc, yo and pull through both loops on hook.

STITCH PATTERNS
SINGLE CROCHET (any number of sts + 1 ch; 1-row repeat)
Row 1: Sc in second ch from hook and in each ch to end, turn.
Row 2: Ch 1, sc in each sc to end, turn.
Repeat Row 2 for Single Crochet.

BORDER POPCORN PATTERN (odd number of sts + 1 ch; 4 rows)
Row 1 (RS): Sc in second ch from hook and in each ch to end, turn.
Row 2: Ch 1, sc in each sc to end, turn.
Row 3: Ch 1, sc in first sc, *popcorn in next sc, sc in next sc; repeat from * to end, turn.
Row 4: Ch 1, sc in each st to end.

CABLE PATTERN (panel of 17 sts; 42 rows)

Note: Ch 1 at the beginning of every row when working Cable Pattern.

Row 1: Sc in first sc, popcorn in next sc, sc in next 4 sc, work FPdc around next sc 2 rows below, FPdc around next popcorn 2 rows below, skip 2 sc behind 2 FPdc just made, sc in next sc, work FPdc around same popcorn as last FPdc, work FPdc around next popcorn 2 rows below, skip 2 sc behind FPdc just made, sc in next 4 sc, popcorn in next sc, sc in last sc.

Row 2 and all WS rows: Sc in each sc across.

Row 3: Sc in first sc, popcorn in next sc, sc in next 3 sc, work FPdc around each of next 2 FPdc 2 rows below, skip 2 sc behind FPdc just made, sc in next sc, popcorn in next sc, sc in next sc, work FPdc around each of next 2 FPdc 2 rows below, skip 2 sc behind FPdc just made, sc in next 3 sc, popcorn in next sc, sc in last sc.

Row 5: Sc in first sc, popcorn in next sc, sc in next 5 sc, work FPdc around each of first 2 FPdc 2 rows below, work FPdc around next 2 FPdc 2 rows below, skip 3 sc behind FPdc just made, sc in next 5 sc, popcorn in next sc, sc in last sc—18 sts.

Row 7: Sc in first sc, popcorn in next sc, sc in next 4 sc, work FPdc around third and fourth FPdc 2 rows below, skip 2 sc behind FPdc just made, sc in next sc, working in front of 2 FPdc just made, work FPdc around each 2 skipped FPdc, skip 3 sc behind FPdc just made, sc in next 4 sc, popcorn in next sc, sc in last sc—17 sts remain.

Row 9: Sc in first sc, popcorn in next sc, sc in next 3 sc, work FPdc around next 2 FPdc 2 rows below, skip 2 sc behind FPdc just made, sc in next 3 sc, work FPdc around next 2 FPdc 2 rows below, skip 2 sc behind FPdc just made, sc in next 3 sc, popcorn in next sc, sc in last sc.

Row 11: Sc in first sc, popcorn in next sc, sc in next 2 sc, work FPdc around next 2 FPdc 2 rows below, skip 2 sc behind FPdc just made, sc in next 5 sc, work FPdc around next 2 FPdc 2 rows below, skip 2 sc behind FPdc just made, sc in next 2 sc, popcorn in next sc, sc in last sc.

Row 13: Sc in first sc, popcorn in next sc, sc in next sc, work FPdc around next 2 FPdc 2 rows below, skip 2 sc behind FPdc just made, sc in next 7 sc, work FPdc around next 2 FPdc, skip 2 sc behind FPdc just made, sc in next sc, popcorn in next sc, sc in last sc.

Row 15: Sc in first sc, popcorn in next sc, sc in next 2 sc, work FPdc around each of first 2 FPdc 2 rows below, skip 2 sc behind FPdc just made, sc in next 5 sc, work 2 FPdc in next 2 FPdc 2 rows below, skip 2 sc behind FPdc just made, sc in next 2 sc, popcorn in next sc, sc in last sc.

Row 17: Sc in first sc, popcorn in next sc, sc in next 3 sc, work FPdc around each of first 2 FPdc 2 rows below, skip 2 sc behind FPdc just made, sc in next 3 sc, work 2 FPdc in next 2 FPdc 2 rows below, skip 2 sc behind FPdc just made, sc in next 3 sc, popcorn in next sc, sc in last sc.

Row 19: Sc in first sc, popcorn in next sc, sc in next 4 sc, work FPdc around each of first 2 FPdc 2 rows below, skip 2 sc behind FPdc just made, sc in next sc, work 2 FPdc in next 2 FPdc 2 rows below, skip 2 sc behind FPdc just made, sc in next 4 sc, popcorn in next sc, sc in last sc.

Row 21: Sc in first sc, popcorn in next sc, sc in next 5 sc, work FPdc around third and fourth FPdc 2 rows below, working in front of FPdc just made, work FPdc decrease, skip 3 sc behind FPdc just made, sc in next 5 sc, popcorn in next sc, sc in last sc.

Row 23: Sc in first sc, popcorn in next sc, sc in next 5 sc, work FPdc around next 2 FPdc 2 rows below, work 2 FPdc around next FPdc decrease 2 rows below, skip 3 sc behind FPdc just made, sc in next 5 sc, popcorn in next sc, sc in last sc—18 sts.

Row 24: Work 1 sc in each st across.

Rows 25-42: Repeat Rows 7-24.

BODY

Note: Sweater is worked back and forth in one piece.
Ch 112 (118, 122, 132, 142, 152).

Begin Border Popcorn Pattern; work even for 3 rows—111 (117, 121, 131, 141, 151) sts remain.

Next Row (WS): Ch 1, sc in each st to last 2 sts, sc2tog over last 2 sts, turn—110 (116, 120, 130, 140, 150) sts remain. Place markers 28 (29, 30, 33, 35, 38) sts in from each edge.

Next Row: Work Cable Pattern over first 17 sts, sc across to last 17 sts, work Cable Pattern to end, turn.

Next Row: Ch 1, sc in each st to end, turn.

SHAPE SIDES

Decrease Row (RS): Work Cable Pattern over 17 sts, [sc across to 2 sts before marker, sc2tog over next 2 sts, sm, sc2tog over next 2 sts], sc across to last 17 sts, work Cable Pattern to end, turn.

Repeat Decrease Row every 6 rows twice, then every 4 rows twice—90 (96, 100, 110, 120, 130) sts remain.

Work even until piece measures approximately 6" from the beginning, ending with a RS row.

SHAPE YOKE

Next Row (WS): Ch 1, sc across to first marker, ch 31 (31, 35, 35, 37, 37) (for first armhole), sc across to second marker, ch 31 (31, 35, 35, 37, 37) (for second armhole), sc in each st to end, turn—152 (158, 170, 180, 194, 204) sts. Work even for body, and for sleeves, begin Border Popcorn Pattern; work even for 4 rows.

Decrease Row 1 (RS): Work Cable Pattern over 17 sts, work 1 (4, 3, 1, 1, 6) sc, sc2tog over next 2 sts, [work 5 sc, sc2tog over next 2 sts] 16 (16, 18, 20, 22, 22) times, work 1 (4, 3, 1, 1, 6) sc, sc2tog over next 2 sts, work Cable Pattern to end, turn —134 (140, 150, 158, 170, 180) sts remain. Work even for 3 rows.

Decrease Row 2 (RS): Work Cable Pattern over 17 sts, work 0 (4, 4, 3, 5, 9) sc, [work 3 sc, sc2tog over next 2 sts] 19 (19, 21, 23, 25, 25) times, work 5 (7, 7, 6, 6, 12) sc, work Cable Pattern to end, turn—115 (121, 129, 135, 145, 155) sts remain. Work even for 1 row.

Decrease Row 3 (RS): Work Cable Pattern over 17 sts, work 1 (4, 4, 3, 4, 9) sc, [sc2tog over next 2 sts, work 2 sc] 20 (20, 22, 24, 26, 26) times, work 0 (3, 3, 2, 3, 8) sc, work Cable Pattern to end, turn—95 (101, 107, 111, 119, 129) sts remain. Work even for 1 row.

Decrease Row 4 (RS): Work Row 3 of Border Popcorn Pattern, dec 10 (12, 14, 16, 20, 24) sts evenly spaced across (by working sc2tog in place of 1 sc), turn—85 (89, 93, 95, 99, 105) sts remain. Work even for 1 (1, 1, 3, 3, 5) row(s).

Buttonhole Row (RS): Ch 1, sc in first 2 sc, ch 2, skip next 2 sc, sc in each sc to end, turn. Work even for 1 row, working 2 sc in ch-2 sp.

Decrease Row 5 (RS): Ch 1, sc in each sc to end, decrease 5 (5, 5, 7, 5, 5) sc evenly spaced across, turn—80 (84, 88, 88, 94, 100) sts remain. Work even for 1 (1, 1, 3, 3, 5) row(s).

Decrease Row 6 (RS): Work 5 (0, 6, 1, 6, 6) sc, [work 2 (2, 1, 2, 1, 1) sc, sc2tog over next 2 sts] 17 (21, 25, 21, 27, 29) times, work 7 (0, 7, 3, 7, 7) sc—63 (63, 63, 67, 67, 71) sts remain. Work even for 1 row.

Next Row (RS): Work Row 3 of Border Popcorn Pattern. Work even for 1 row.
Repeat Buttonhole Row. Work even for 1 row, working 2 sc in ch-2 sp.
Fasten off.

FINISHING

Fold first 2 Border Popcorn Pattern to WS and sew in place, being careful not to let sts show on RS. Sew buttons opposite buttonholes.

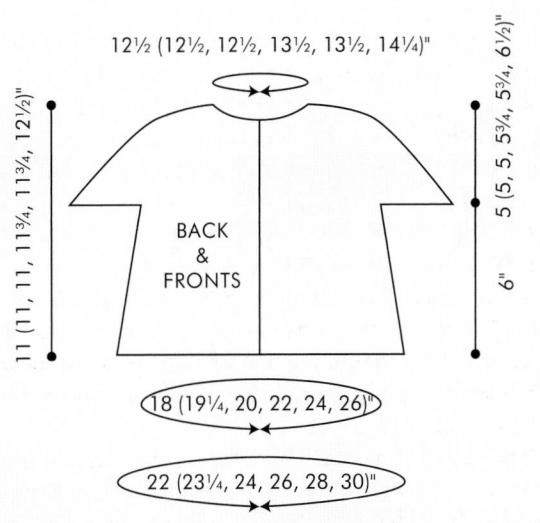

12½ (12½, 12½, 13½, 13½, 14¼)"

11 (11, 11, 11¾, 11¾, 12½)"

5 (5, 5, 5¾, 5¾, 6½)"

6"

BACK & FRONTS

18 (19¼, 20, 22, 24, 26)"

22 (23¼, 24, 26, 28, 30)"

Key Lime Blanket

This simple, fresh baby blanket is created by combining two-by-two rib and Garter stitch in concentric circles. Worked from the center outward, all the increases occur on knit rounds, which makes the counting easy to manage. The off-white center and border mimic the look of a sliced lime.

FINISHED MEASUREMENTS
36" diameter

YARN
Berroco Vintage Chunky (50% acrylic / 40% wool / 10% nylon; 100 grams / 130 yards): 6 hanks #6124 Kiwi (MC); 2 hanks #6101 Mochi (A)

NEEDLES
One 36" (90 cm) long circular (circ) needle size US 10 (6 mm)
One set of five double-pointed needles (dpn) size US 10 (6 mm)
Change needle size if necessary to obtain correct gauge.

NOTIONS
Stitch marker

GAUGE
14 sts and 21 rows = 4" (10 cm) in Stockinette stitch (St st)

BLANKET
Using dpns and A, CO 8 sts. Divide sts evenly among 4 dpns. Join for working in the rnd; pm for beginning of rnd.
Note: Change to circ needle when necessary for number of sts on needles.
Rnd 1: *K1-tbl; repeat from * to end.
Rnd 2: *K1, M1; repeat from * to end—16 sts.
Rnd 3: Knit.
Rnd 4: Repeat Rnd 2—32 sts.
Rnd 5: Purl.
Rnd 6: Knit.
Rnd 7: Purl.
Rnd 8: *K2, M1; repeat from * to end—48 sts.
Rnds 9 and 11: Knit.
Rnds 10 and 12: Purl.
Rnd 13: *K4, M1; repeat from * to end—60 sts.
Rnds 14-18: *K2, p2; repeat from * to end.
Rnd 19: Change to MC; knit.
Rnd 20: *K15, M1; repeat from * to end—64 sts.
Rnd 21: Purl.
Rnd 22: Knit.
Rnd 23: Purl.
Rnd 24: *K2, M1; repeat from * to end—96 sts.
Rnds 25-29: *K2, p2; repeat from * to end.
Rnd 30: *K3, M1; repeat from * to end—128 sts.
Rnd 31: Purl.
Rnd 32: Knit.
Rnd 33: Purl.

Rnd 34: *K4, M1; repeat from * to end—160 sts.

Rnds 35-41: *K2, p2; repeat from * to end.

Rnd 42: *K5, M1; repeat from * to end—192 sts.

Rnd 43: Purl.

Rnd 44: Knit.

Rnd 45: Purl.

Rnd 46: *K6, M1; repeat from * to end—224 sts.

Rnds 47-55: *K2, p2; repeat from * to end.

Rnd 56: *K7, M1; repeat from * to end—256 sts.

Rnd 57: Purl.

Rnd 58: Knit.

Rnd 59: Purl.

Rnd 60: *K8, M1; repeat from * to end—288 sts.

Rnds 61-71: *K2, p2; repeat from * to end.

Rnd 72: *K9, M1; repeat from * to end—320 sts.

Rnd 73: Purl.

Rnd 74: Knit.

Rnd 75: Purl.

Rnd 76: *K10, M1; repeat from * to end—352 sts.

Rnds 77-89: *K2, p2; repeat from * to end.

Rnd 90: *K11, M1; repeat from * to end—384 sts.

Rnd 91: Purl.

Rnd 92: Knit.

Rnd 93: Purl.

Rnd 94: *K12, M1; repeat from * to end—416 sts.

Rnds 95-109: *K2, p2; repeat from * to end.

Rnds 110-116: Change to A; *k2, p2; repeat from * to end.

Rnd 117: Knit.

Rnd 118: Purl.

Rnd 119: Knit.

Rnd 120: Purl. BO all sts knitwise.

FINISHING

Block lightly (see Special Techniques, page 156).

Orangelo
Bib

This bib is sweet and bright like its namesake fruit, and it is even worked in "segments." Decreases are worked at the edges of each segment, bringing each one to a point.

FINISHED MEASUREMENTS

9½ (11)" diameter at widest point

YARN

Berroco Comfort Chunky (50% super fine nylon / 50% super fine acrylic; 100 grams / 150 yards): 1 skein #5724 Pumpkin

NEEDLES

One pair straight needles size US 10½ (6.5 mm)
Change needle size if necessary to obtain correct gauge.

NOTIONS

Stitch markers

GAUGE

14 sts and 20 rows = 4" (10 cm) in Stockinette stitch (St st)

BIB

Using Long-Tail CO (see Special Techniques, page 156), CO 86 (100) sts.

Decrease Row 1 (RS): K1, [k2tog, k8 (10) sts, ssk, pm] 7 times, k1—72 (86) sts remain. Knit 5 rows.

Decrease Row 2 (RS): Change to St st. Decrease 14 sts this row, then every 4 rows 3 (4) times, as follows: K1, [k2tog, knit to 2 sts before marker, ssk, sm] 7 times, k1—16 sts remain. Work even for 3 rows, removing markers.

Decrease Row 3 (RS): K1, [k2tog] 7 times, k1—9 sts remain. Work even for 1 row.

Decrease Row 4 (RS): [K3tog] 3 times—3 sts remain. BO all sts.

TIE

Using Knitted or Cable CO (see Special Techniques, page 156), CO 34 (40) sts, turn so that CO sts are on right-hand needle. With RS of Bib facing, pick up and knit 1 st at corner of CO edge and right side edge, pass next st (last CO st) over picked-up st, pick up and knit 33 (39) sts along side edge, BO edge, then other side edge, turn—67 (79) sts.

Next Row: Using Knitted or Cable CO, CO 33 (39) sts, knit to end—100 (118) sts. BO all sts purlwise.

Darla Blanket

When my Gram was a young mother in the 1930s, money was tight, materials were scarce, and innovative reuse was the rule of the day. Dresses, blouses, and petticoats, once worn out or outgrown, were usually refashioned into coverlets. This blanket takes a cue from quilts of that era, using a variety of stitches and colors to simulate patchwork squares of calico and gingham. The squares are then pieced together in a casual, random order.

FINISHED MEASUREMENTS
Blanket: 35" wide x 45" long
Square: 5" x 5"

YARN
Berroco Comfort (50% super fine nylon / 50% super fine acrylic; 100 grams / 210 yards): 3 skeins each #9703 Barley (A) and #9749 Aunt Abby Rose (B); 1 skein each #9748 Aunt Martha Green (C), #9746 Iron Oxide (D), #9758 Crypto Crystalline (E), and #9714 Robin's Egg (F)

CROCHET HOOKS
Crochet hook size US H/8 (5 mm)
Crochet hook size US I/9 (5.5 mm)
Crochet hook size US J/10 (6 mm)
Change hook size if necessary to obtain correct gauge.

GAUGE
14 sts and 18 rows = 4" (10 cm) in Single Crochet (sc), using smallest crochet hook

SQUARE 1 (make 9)
Using size I/9 crochet hook and A, ch 22.
Row 1: Work 3 dc in 6th ch from hook, *ch 1, skip next 3 ch sts, 3 dc in next ch; repeat from * to end, ending last repeat with 2 dc in last ch, turn.
Row 2: Ch 2, *dc in next ch-1 sp, tr in next corresponding skipped ch in foundation ch, dc in same ch-1 sp in current row, ch 1; repeat from * to end, ending with 2 dc in top of beginning ch, turn.
Row 3: Ch 2, *dc in next ch-1 sp, working over ch-1 sp, tr in next corresponding st 2 rows below, dc in same ch-1 sp in current row, ch 1; repeat from * to end, ending with 2 dc in top of turning ch, turn.
Repeat Row 3 eleven times. Fasten off.

SQUARE 2 (make 9)
Work as for Square 1, using B.

SQUARE 3 (make 9)
Note: When changing colors, work to last dc, yo, pull up a loop in last dc, yo and pull through 2 loops on hook, then yo with new color and pull through all loops on hook. Do not cut yarn at end of rows, but carry loosely up side.
Using size I/9 crochet hook and C, ch 22. Complete as for Square 1, alternating 1 row each in C, B, then D.

ASSEMBLY DIAGRAM

KEY

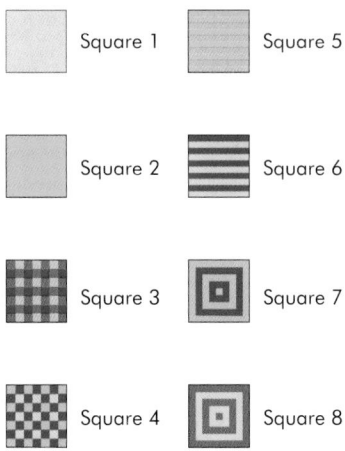

SQUARE 4 (make 6)
Work as for Square 3, using A, E, and F in place of C, B, and D, respectively.

SQUARE 5 (make 6)
Using largest crochet hook and B, ch 16.
Row 1: Sc in 2nd ch from hook and in next 2 ch, *dc in next 3 ch, sc in next 3 ch; repeat from * to end. Do not break yarn; turn.
Row 2: Change to A. Ch 3, sk first sc, dc in next 2 sc, *sc in next 3 dc, dc in next 3 sc; repeat from * to end, pull up a long loop in last st. Do not turn. Remove hook from long loop and return to beginning of row just worked.
Row 3: Pull color B (from 2 rows below) through top of begin-ning ch and sc in same st, sc in next 2 dc, *dc in next 3 sc, sc in next 3 dc; repeat from * to last st, insert hook through long loop from Row 2, shorten this loop and yo with A, pull through 2 loops on hook, and turn.
Repeat Rows 2 and 3 five times, then repeat Row 2 once.
Fasten off.

SQUARE 6 (make 9)
Using largest crochet hook and F, ch 16.
Work as for Square 5, using F and E instead of B and A.

SQUARE 7 (make 6)
Using smallest crochet hook and A, begin with a sliding loop.
Rnd 1 (RS): Ch 3, work 2 dc in loop, ch 2, *work 3 dc in loop, ch 2; repeat from * twice, join with a slip st in top of beginning ch. Fasten off.
Rnd 2: With RS facing, join D with a slip st in any ch-2 sp. Ch 3, [2 dc, ch 2, 3 dc] in same ch-2 sp, ch 1, *[3 dc, ch 2, 3 dc] in next ch-2 sp, ch 1; repeat from * twice, join with a slip st to top of beginning ch.
Rnd 3: With RS facing, join A with a slip st in any ch-2 sp. Ch 3, [2 dc, ch 2, 3 dc] in same ch-2 sp, ch 1, 3 dc in next ch-1 sp, ch 1, *[3 dc, ch-2, 3 dc] in next ch-2 sp, ch 1, 3 dc in ch-1 sp, ch 1; repeat from * twice, join with a slip st in top of beginning ch 3. Fasten off.

Rnd 4: With RS facing, join D with a slip st in any ch-2 sp. Ch 3, [2 dc, ch 2, 3 dc] in same ch-2 sp, ch 1, [3 dc in ch-1 sp, ch 1] twice, *[3 dc, ch 2, 3 dc] in next ch-2 sp, ch 1, [3 dc in ch-1 sp, ch 1] twice; repeat from * twice, join with a slip st in top of beginning ch.

Rnd 5: With RS facing, join A with a slip st in any ch-2 sp. Ch 3, [2 dc, ch 2, 3 dc] in same ch-2 sp, ch 1, [3 dc in ch-1 sp, ch 1] 3 times, *[3 dc, ch 2, 3 dc] in next ch-2 sp, ch 1, [3 dc in ch-1 sp, ch 1] 3 times; repeat from * twice, join with a slip st in top of beginning ch. Fasten off.

SQUARE 8 (make 9)
Work as for Square 7, using C and E instead of A and D.

FINISHING
Using A, sew Squares together according to Assembly Diagram. Make sure to work over any long loops on side caused by carrying yarn up.

BORDER
With RS facing, using smallest crochet hook, join A in any corner, ch 1, *3 sc in corner st, sc evenly to next corner; repeat from * around entire Blanket, join with a slip st in first sc. Fasten off.

Block lightly (see Special Techniques, page 156).

Paddington Coat

This little hooded coat is a checkerboard of cables. The circular elements play with scale—big Os form figure eights, while the little Os alternate with bobbles. The bobbles are worked without turning, so they are particularly easy to make, and the I-cord edge is worked as you go, so there is no fussy finishing.

SIZES
3 (6, 9, 12, 18, 24) months

FINISHED MEASUREMENTS
18½ (19, 20, 22½, 24, 26½)" chest

YARN
Berroco Comfort (50% super fine nylon / 50% super fine acrylic; 100 grams / 210 yards): 2 (3, 3, 3, 3, 4) skeins #9716 Chambray

NEEDLES
One pair straight needles size US 8 (5 mm)
One pair straight needles size US 6 (4 mm)
One pair straight needles size US 7 (4.5 mm)
Change needle size if necessary to obtain correct gauge.

NOTIONS
Stitch markers, including 1 removable marker; cable needle (cn); stitch holder; six ⅝" buttons

GAUGE
20 sts and 28 rows = 4" (10 cm) in Moss stitch, using largest needles

ABBREVIATION
K1-f/b/f: Knit into front, back, then front loop of same st to increase two sts.

STITCH PATTERNS
1X1 RIB (odd number of sts; 1-row repeat)
Row 1 (RS): K1, *p1, k1; repeat from * to end.
Row 2: Knit the knit sts and purl the purl sts as they face you. Repeat Row 2 for 1x1 Rib.

MOSS STITCH (any number of sts; 4-row repeat)
Row 1: *K1, p1; repeat from * to end, end k1 if an odd number of sts.
Row 2: Knit the knit sts and purl the purl sts as they face you.
Row 3: Purl the knit sts and knit the purl sts as they face you.
Row 4: Repeat Row 2.
Repeat Rows 1-4 for Moss st.

BACK
Using smallest needles, CO 57 (59, 61, 67, 71, 77) sts. Begin 1x1 Rib; work even for 6 rows.
Next Row (RS): Change to largest needles. Work 7 (8, 9, 12, 14, 17) sts in Moss st, work Row 1 of Cable Pattern from chart over next 20 sts, pm, work Moss st over next 3 sts, pm, work Row 17 of Cable Pattern over next 20 sts, pm, work 7 (8, 9, 12, 14, 17) sts in Moss st. Work even until piece measures 10 (11, 11, 12, 12, 13)" from the beginning, ending with a WS row. BO 17 (18, 19, 20, 22, 24) sts at the beginning of the next 2 rows. Place remaining 23 (23, 23, 27, 27, 29) sts on st holder.

LEFT FRONT
Using smallest needles, CO 29 (29, 31, 33, 35, 39) sts.
Row 1 (RS): P1, *k1, p1; repeat from * to last 2 sts, k2.
Row 2: Slip 2 sts, k1, *p1, k1; repeat from * to end.

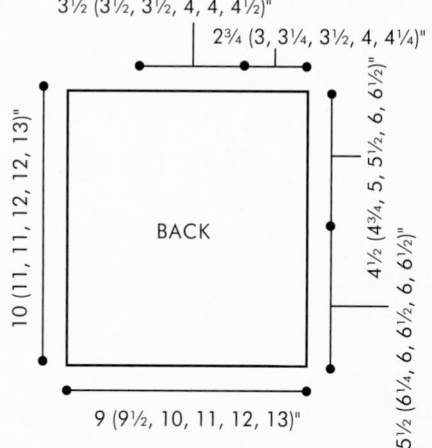

3½ (3½, 3½, 4, 4, 4½)"

2¾ (3, 3¼, 3½, 4, 4¼)"

10 (11, 11, 12, 12, 13)"

BACK

4½ (4¾, 5, 5½, 6, 6½)"

5½ (6¼, 6, 6½, 6, 6½)"

9 (9½, 10, 11, 12, 13)"

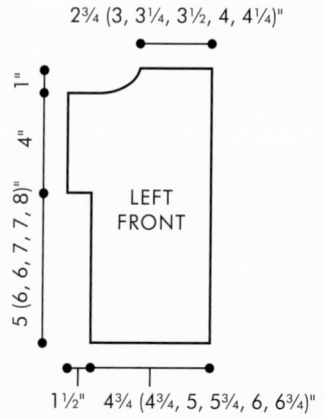

2¾ (3, 3¼, 3½, 4, 4¼)"

1"

4"

5 (6, 6, 7, 7, 8)"

LEFT FRONT

1½"   4¾ (4¾, 5, 5¾, 6, 6¾)"

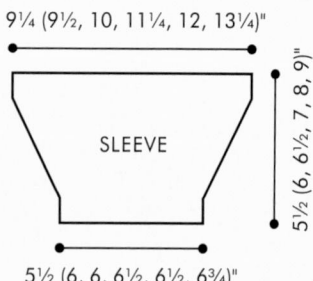

9¼ (9½, 10, 11¼, 12, 13¼)"

5½ (6, 6½, 7, 8, 9)"

SLEEVE

5½ (6, 6, 6½, 6½, 6¾)"

Repeat Rows 1 and 2 three times, increasing 0 (1, 0, 1, 1, 0) st(s) on last row—29 (30, 31, 34, 36, 39).

Row 9: Change to largest needle. Work 7 (8, 9, 12, 14, 17) sts in Moss st, pm, work Row 1 of Cable Pattern over next 20 sts, k2.

Row 10: Slip 2, work to end.

Work even until piece measures 5 (6, 6, 7, 7, 8)" from the beginning, ending with a WS row.

SHAPE PLACKET

Row 1 (RS): Work to end, CO 7 sts—36 (37, 38, 41, 43, 46) sts.

Row 2: Slip 2 sts, work Moss st over next 7 sts, work to end.

Row 3: Work to last 9 sts, work Moss st to last 2 sts, k2.

Work even until piece measures 9 (10, 10, 11, 11, 12)" from the beginning, ending with a RS row.

SHAPE NECK

Next Row (WS): BO 11 (11, 11, 13, 13, 14) sts at neck edge once, then 4 sts once, then decrease 1 st at neck edge every row 4 times, as follows: On RS rows, work to last 2 sts, k2tog; on WS rows, p2tog, work to end—17 (18, 19, 20, 22, 24) sts. BO all sts.

RIGHT FRONT

Work as for Left Front, reversing st patterns and shaping, and beginning Cable Pattern with Row 17, until 4 rows of Placket have been completed.

Buttonhole Row (RS): Work 3 sts, yo, work 2 sts together (k2tog if next st to be worked is a purl st, or p2tog if next st to be worked is a knit st), work 5 sts, yo, work 2 sts together, work to end. Complete as for Left Front, working Buttonhole Row every 10 rows twice more.

SLEEVES

Using smallest needles, CO 35 (37, 37, 39, 39, 41) sts. Begin 1x1 Rib; work even for 6 rows, decreasing 7 sts evenly on last row—28 (30, 30, 32, 32, 34) sts remain.

Next Row (RS): Change to largest needles and Moss st; work even for 2 rows.

SHAPE SLEEVE

Next Row (RS): Increase 1 st each side this row, every other row 6 (3, 4, 7, 6, 7) times, then every 4 rows 2 (5, 5, 4, 7, 8) times—46 (48, 50, 56, 60, 66) sts. Work even until piece measures 5½ (6, 6½, 7, 8, 9)" from the beginning. BO all sts.

FINISHING

Sew shoulder seams.

HOOD

With RS facing, using smallest needle and beginning at Right Front after placket, pick up and knit 18 (18, 18, 20, 20, 22) sts along Right Front neck edge to shoulder, k23 (23, 23, 27, 27, 29) from st holder for Back neck, pick up and knit 18 (18, 18, 20, 20, 22) sts along Left Front neck edge to placket—59 (59, 59, 67, 67, 73) sts.

KEY

□	Knit on RS, purl on WS.
⊡	Purl on RS, knit on WS.
●	Make Knot: Knit in front, back, front of st, slip first 2 sts over last st
⧖	K1-tbl
⬚	Slip 1 st to cn, hold to back, k1, k1 from cn.
⬚	Slip 1 st to cn, hold to front, k1, k1 from cn.
⬚	Slip 2 sts to cn, hold to back, k2, k2 from cn.
⬚	Slip 2 sts to cn, hold to front, k2, k2 from cn.

CABLE PATTERN

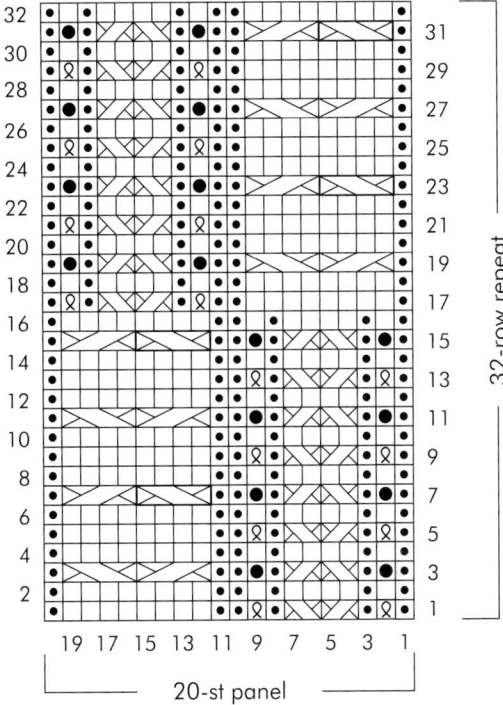

20-st panel — 32-row repeat

Row 1 (WS): Slip 2 sts, work in Moss st to last 2 sts, slip 2 sts.

Row 2: K2, work to last 2 sts, k2.

Work even for 3 rows.

SHAPE HOOD

Next Row (RS): Change to size US 7 needles. Work 10 (10, 10, 14, 14, 16) sts, k1-f/b/f, work to last 11 (11, 11, 15, 15, 17) sts, k1-f/b/f, work to end—63 (63, 63, 71, 71, 77) sts. Working increased sts in Moss st, work even until piece measures 6" from pick-up row, ending with a WS row. Place removable marker on center st.

Next Row: Decrease 2 sts this row, every 4 rows once, then every other row 3 times, as follows: Work to 1 st before center st, work 3 sts together (k3tog if next st to be worked is a purl st, or p3tog if next st to be worked is a knit st), work to end—53 (53, 53, 61, 61, 67) sts remain. Work even for 1 row.

Next Row: Work to 1 st before center st, work 2 sts together in pattern, work to end—52 (52, 52, 60, 60, 66) sts remain. Work even for 1 row. Transfer 26 (26, 26, 30, 30, 33) sts to each of 2 needles. Using Three-Needle BO (see Special Techniques, page 156), BO all sts.

Place markers 4½ (4¾, 5, 5½, 6, 6½)" down from shoulders on Back and Front.

Sew Sleeves between markers. Sew side and Sleeve seams.

Sew buttons to Left Front Placket opposite buttonholes.

Snowflake Blanket

Arches of raised crochet stitches come together to form cabled hexagons in this highly textured blanket. The hexagon motif by itself is pretty, but when repeated, it becomes a stunning network of elaborate snowflakes.

FINISHED MEASUREMENTS
Blanket: 33" wide x 45" long
Hexagon: 11" wide

YARN
Berroco Comfort DK (50% super fine nylon / 50% super fine acrylic; 50 grams / 178 yards): 12 skeins #2703 Barley

CROCHET HOOKS
Crochet hook size US G/6 (4 mm)
Change hook size if necessary to obtain correct gauge.

GAUGE
20 sts and 10 rows = 4" (10 cm) in Double Crochet (dc)

ABBREVIATIONS
FPdc: Yo, insert hook from front to back to front around post of next dc, yo and pull up a loop, [yo and pull through 2 loops on hook] twice.
BPdc: Yo, insert hook from back to front to back around post of next dc, yo and pull up a loop, [yo and pull through 2 loops on hook] twice.

HEXAGON (make 13)
Begin with a sliding loop.

Rnd 1: Ch 6 (counts as tr and ch-2), tr in ring, *ch-2, tr in ring; repeat from * 9 times, join with hdc to fourth ch of beginning ch-6 instead of last ch-2 sp—12 tr.

Rnd 2: Ch 6 (counts as dc and ch-3 here and throughout), dc in sp made by joining hdc, *dc in next tr, dc in next ch-2 sp, dc in next tr**, [dc, ch 3, dc] in next ch-2 sp; repeat from * to end, ending last repeat at **, join with a slip st in third ch of beginning ch-6—30 dc and 6 ch-3 sps.

Rnd 3: Slip st in next ch-3 sp, ch 6, dc in same sp, *[ch 1, skip 1 dc, dc in next dc] twice, ch 1**, [dc, ch 3, dc] in next ch-3 sp; repeat from * to end, ending last repeat at **, join with a slip st in third ch of beginning ch-6.

Rnd 4: Ch 3 (counts as dc), *[dc, ch 3, dc] in next ch-3 sp, [dc in next dc, dc in next ch-1 sp] 3 times, dc in next dc; repeat from * to end, omitting last dc, join with a slip st in top of beginning ch-3.

Rnd 5: Slip st in next ch-3 sp, ch 6, dc in same ch-3 sp, *dc in next 9 dc**, [dc, ch 3, dc] in next ch-3 sp; repeat from * to end, ending last repeat at **, join with a slip st in third ch of beginning ch-6.

Rnd 6: Slip st in next ch-3 sp, ch 6 (counts as dc and ch-3), dc in same ch-3 sp, *dc in next dc, FPdc in next 2 dc, dc in next 5 dc, FPdc in next 2 dc**, dc in next dc, [dc, ch 3, dc] in next ch-3 sp; repeat from * to end, ending last repeat at **, join with a slip st in third ch of beginning ch-6.

Rnd 7: Slip st in next ch-3 sp, ch 6, dc in same ch-3 sp, *dc in next 2 dc, skip next 2 FPdc, dc in next dc, working in front of dc just worked, FPdc in 2 skipped FPdc, dc in next 3 dc, skip next dc, FPdc in next 2 FPdc, working in back of FPdc just

worked, dc in last skipped dc, dc in next 2 dc**, [dc, ch 3, dc] in next ch-3 sp; repeat from * to end, ending last repeat at **, join with a slip st in third ch of beginning ch-6.

Rnd 8: Slip st in next ch-3 sp, ch 6, dc in same ch-3 sp, *dc in next 4 dc, skip next 2 FPdc, dc in next dc, working in front of dc just worked, FPdc in 2 skipped FPdc, dc in next dc, skip next dc, FPdc in next 2 FPdc, working in back of FPdc just worked, dc in last skipped dc, dc in next 4 dc**, [dc, ch 3, dc] in next ch-3 sp; repeat from * to end, ending last repeat at **, join with a slip st in third ch of beginning ch-6.

Rnd 9: Slip st in next ch-3 sp, ch 6, dc in same ch-3 sp, *dc in next 6 dc, skip next 2 FPdc and next dc, FPdc in next 2 FPdc, working in back of 2 FPdc just worked, dc in last skipped dc, working in front of 2 FPdc just worked, work FPdc in 2 skipped FPdc, dc in next 6 dc**, [dc, ch 3, dc] in next ch-3 sp; repeat from * to end, ending last repeat at **, join with a slip st in third ch of beginning ch-6.

Rnd 10: Slip st in next ch-3 sp, ch 6, dc in same ch-3 sp, *dc in next 7 dc, FPdc in next 2 FPdc, dc in next dc, FPdc in next 2 FPdc, dc in next 7 dc **, [dc, ch 3, dc] in next ch-3 sp; repeat from * to end, ending last repeat at **, join with a slip st in third ch of beginning ch-6.

Rnd 11: Slip st in next ch-3 sp, ch 6, dc in same ch-3 sp, *dc in next 8 dc, skip next 2 FPdc and next dc, FPdc in next 2 FPdc, working in back of 2 FPdc just worked, dc in last skipped dc, working in front of 2 FPdc just worked, work FPdc in 2 skipped FPdc, dc in next 8 dc**, [dc, ch 3, dc] in next ch-3 sp; repeat from * to end, ending last repeat at **, join with a slip st in third ch of beginning ch-6.

Rnd 12: Slip st in next ch-3 sp, ch 1, 5 sc in same ch-3 sp, *sc in each st to next ch-3 sp (23 sc)**, 5 sc in next ch-3 sp; repeat from * to end, ending last repeat at **, join with a slip st in first sc.

Rnd 13: Ch 4 (counts as dc and ch-1), skip first 1 sc, *[dc, ch 3, dc] in next sc (center sc of 5 sc corner), ch 1, skip next sc, [dc in next sc, ch 1, skip next sc] across to next corner sc; repeat from * to end, join with a slip st in third ch of beginning ch-4.

Rnd 14: Ch 1, sc in each dc and ch-1 sp around, working 5 sc in each ch-3 corner, join with a slip st in first sc. Fasten off, leaving a tail long enough to sew Hexagon to next Hexagon.

HALF HEXAGON (make 4)

Note: Half Hexagon is worked back and forth through Row 11, then worked in the rnd for Rnds 12-14.

Begin with a sliding loop.

Row 1 (WS): Ch 6 (counts as tr and ch-2), tr in ring, *ch 2, tr in ring; repeat from * 3 times, turn—6 tr.

Row 2: Ch 3 (counts as 1 dc), dc in first tr, dc in next ch-2 sp, dc in next tr, [dc, ch 3, dc] in next ch-2 sp, dc in tr, dc in next ch-2 sp, dc in next tr, [dc, ch 3, dc] in next ch-2 sp, dc in next tr, dc in next ch-2 sp, 2 dc in third ch of turning ch, turn—15 dc and 2 ch-3 sps.

Row 3: Ch 4 (counts as dc and ch-1), skip first 2 dc, dc in next dc, ch 1, skip next dc, dc in next dc, ch 1, [dc, ch 3, dc] in next ch-3 sp, [ch 1, skip next dc, dc in next dc] twice, ch 1, [dc, ch 3, dc] in next ch-3 sp, [ch 1, skip next dc, dc in next dc] twice, ch 1, dc in top of turning ch, turn.

Row 4: Ch 3 (counts as dc here and throughout), dc in first dc, *dc in each dc and ch-1 sp to next ch-3 sp, [dc, ch 3, dc] in next ch-3 sp; repeat from * once, [dc in next dc, dc in next ch-1 sp] 3 times, 2 dc in third ch of turning ch, turn.

Row 5: Ch 3, dc in first dc, dc in next 8 dc, [dc, ch 3, dc] in next ch-3 sp, dc in next 9 dc, [dc, ch 3, dc] in next ch-3 sp, dc in next 8 dc, 2 dc in top of turning ch, turn.

Row 6: Ch 3, dc in first dc, *FPdc in next 2 dc, dc in next 5 dc, FPdc in next 2 dc**, dc in next dc, [dc, ch 3, dc] in next ch-3 sp, dc in next dc; repeat from * once, then repeat from * to ** once, 2 dc in top of turning ch, turn.

Row 7: Ch 3, dc in first dc, *dc in next dc, skip next 2 FPdc, dc in next dc, working in back of dc just worked, BPdc in 2 skipped FPdc, dc in next 3 dc, skip next dc, BPdc in next 2 FPdc, working in front of 2 BPdc just worked, dc in last skipped dc**, dc in next 2 dc, [dc, ch 3, dc] in next ch-3 sp, dc in next dc; repeat from * once, then repeat from * to ** once, dc in next dc, 2 dc in top of turning ch, turn.

Row 8: Ch 3, dc in first dc, *dc in next 3 dc, skip next 2 BPdc, dc in next dc, working in front of dc just worked, FPdc in 2 skipped BPdc, dc in next dc, skip next dc, FPdc in next 2 BPdc, working in back of FPdcs just worked, dc in skipped dc**, dc in next 4 dc, [dc, ch 3, dc] in ch-3 sp, dc in next dc; repeat from * once, then repeat from * to ** once, dc in next 3 dc, 2 dc in top of turning ch, turn.

Row 9: Ch 3, dc in first dc, *dc in next 5 dc, skip next 2 FPdc and next dc, work BPdc in next 2 FPdc, working in back of 2 BPdc just worked, dc in skipped dc, working under last 2 BPdc worked, BPdc in last 2 skipped FPdc**, dc in next 6 dc, [dc, ch 3, dc] in ch-3 sp, dc in next dc; repeat from * once, then repeat from * to ** once, dc in next 5 dc, 2 dc in top of turning ch, turn.

Row 10: Ch 3, dc in first dc, *dc in next 6 dc, FPdc in next 2 BPdc, dc in next dc, FPdc in next 2 BPdc, **dc in next 7 dc, [dc, ch 3, dc] in ch-3 sp, dc in next dc; repeat from * once, then repeat from * to ** once, dc in next 6 dc, 2 dc in top of turning ch, turn.

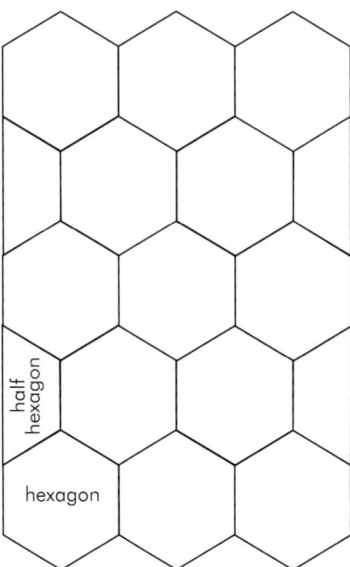

Row 11: Ch 3, dc in first dc, *dc in next 7 dc, skip next 2 FPdc and next dc, BPdc in next 2 FPdc, working in back of 2 BPdc just worked, dc in last skipped dc, working under last 2 BPdc worked, BPdc in last 2 skipped FPdc**, dc in next 8 dc, [dc, ch 3, dc] in ch-3 sp, dc in next dc; repeat from * once, then repeat from * to ** once, dc in next 7 dc, 2 dc in top of turning ch, turn.

Rnd 12: *Note: Change to working in the rnd.* Ch 1, *sc in each dc and BPdc across to next ch-3 sp, 5 sc in ch-3 sp; repeat from * once, then sc in each dc and BPdc to end of row, ending with sc in top of turning ch. Do not turn; work 46 sc evenly spaced across straight edge of motif, join with a slip st in beginning sc.

Rnd 13: Ch 4 (counts as 1 dc and ch-1), skip 1 sc, *[dc in next sc, ch 1, skip next sc] to next corner sc, **[dc, ch 3, dc] in corner sc, ch 1; repeat from * 2 times, then rep from * to ** once, end dc in last corner, ch 3, join with a slip st in third ch of beginning ch-4.

Rnd 14: Ch 1, sc in each dc and ch-1 around, working 5 sc in each ch-3 corner sp, join with a slip st in first sc. Fasten off, leaving a tail long enough to sew Half Hexagon to next Hexagon.

FINISHING

Sew Hexagons together through back loops, following Assembly Diagram.

Block lightly (see Special Techniques, page 156).

Slice Cap

This basic cap can be made two ways—as a play on a traditional baseball cap (see right), and as a 1940s-inspired ruffled-brim cap (see below). The crown of both caps is comprised of six slices worked in cheerful alternating colors.

Approximately 15" circumference

YARN
Baseball Cap
Berroco Comfort (50% super fine nylon / 50% super fine acrylic; 100 grams / 210 yards): 1 skein each #9747 Cadet (A) and #9729 Smokestack (B)

Ruffled Cap
Berroco Vintage (50% acrylic / 40% wool / 10% nylon; 100 grams / 217 yards): 1 hank each #51180 Grapefruit (A) and #51179 Apricot (B)

CROCHET HOOKS
One crochet hook size US G/6 (4 mm)
Change hook size if necessary to obtain correct gauge.

GAUGE
18 sts and 22 rows = 4" (10 cm) in Single Crochet (sc)

WEDGE 1
Set-Up Row: Using A, ch 23. Sc in second ch and in each ch to end, turn—22 sc.
Row 1: Ch 1, sc in next 18 sc, slip st in last sc, turn.
Row 2: Ch 1, skip slip st, sc in each sc to end, turn—18 sc remain.
Row 3: Ch 1, sc in next 14 sc, work slip st in next sc, turn.
Row 4: Ch 1, skip slip st, sc in each sc to end, turn—14 sc remain.
Row 5: Ch 1, sc in next 10 sc, slip st in next sc, turn.
Row 6: Ch 1, skip slip st, sc in each sc to end, turn—10 sc remain.

Row 7: Ch 1, sc in next 10 sc, sc in next slip st, slip st in next sc, turn.

Row 8: Ch 1, skip slip st, sc in each sc to end, turn—11 sc.

Row 9: Ch 1, sc in next 11 sc, sc in next slip st, sc in next 2 sc, sc in next slip st, slip st in next sc, turn.

Row 10: Ch 1, skip slip st, sc in each sc to end, turn—15 sc.

Row 11: Ch 1, sc in next 15 sc, sc in next slip st, sc in next 2 sc, sc in next slip st, slip st in next sc, turn.

Row 12: Ch 1, skip slip st, sc in each sc to end, turn—19 sc.

Row 13: Ch 1, sc in next 19 sc, sc in next slip st, sc in next 2 sc, slip st in ch 1 from the first row, turn.

Row 14: Ch 1, skip slip st, sc in each sc to end, turn—22 sc.

WEDGE 2

Using B, sc in next 21 sc, slip st in last sc.

Next row: Ch 1, skip slip st, sc in each sc to end, turn—21 sc.

Work Rows 1-14 as for Wedge 1.

WEDGES 3-6

Alternating colors A and B, work 4 more Wedges as for Wedge 2. Join Wedge 6 to Wedge 1 with a row of slip st.

FINISHING

BASEBALL CAP

Band: Using A, work 66 sc around bottom edge. Work 3 more rnds sc.

Split Band: Sc in next 19 sc, working from left to right, work Rev sc over last 42 sts. Fasten off.

Brim: Return to unfinished 24 sts. Mark center 16 sts.

With RS facing, using B, join yarn with a slip st to beginning of center 16 sts.

Row 1: Ch 1, [1 sc, 2 sc in next sc, 1 sc] 5 times, 1 sc in last sc—21 sc. Slip st in next sc of Band, turn.

Rows 2 and 3: Ch 1, work 2 sc in slip st, sc to end of Brim, slip st in next st on Band—25 sc.

Rows 4 and 5: Ch 1, work 2 sc in slip st, work 2 sc in next sc, sc to end of Brim, slip st in next st on Band—31 sc.

Rows 6 and 7: Ch 1, work 2 sc in slip st, work sc in next sc, work 2 sc in next sc, sc to end of Brim, slip st in next sc on Band—37 sc. Working from left to right, ch 1, work Rev sc to end of Brim. Fasten off.

RUFFLED CAP

Band: Using A, work 66 sc around bottom edge. Work 3 more rnds sc.

Split Band: Sc in next 8 sc, working from left to right, work Rev sc over last 16 sts. Fasten off.

Brim: Return to unfinished 50 sts. Mark center 42 sts.

With RS facing, using B, join yarn with a slip st to beginning of center 42 sts. Ch 1, sc to end, turn—42 sc.

Row 1: Ch 1, sc in each sc to end of Brim, work slip st in next sc on Band, turn.

Row 2: Ch 1, sc in slip st, *work 2 sc in next sc, sc in next 2 sc; repeat from * to end of Brim, slip st in next sc on Band, turn—57 sc.

Row 3: Ch 1, sc in slip st and in each sc to end, slip st in next sc on Band, turn—58 sc.

Row 4: Ch 1, sc in slip st, *work 2 sc in next sc, sc in next 2 sc; repeat from *, end sc in last sc of Brim, slip st in next sc on Band, turn—78 sc.

Row 5: Repeat Row 3—79 sc.

Rows 6 and 7: Repeat Rows 4 and 5—107 sc.

Row 8: Ch 1, sc in slip st, *work 2 sc in next sc, sc in next 2 sc; repeat from *, end sc in last 2 sc of Brim—144 sc.

Working from left to right, ch 1, work Rev sc to end of Brim. Fasten off.

Weave in all loose ends.

"Smocked"
Cardigan

In this classic cardigan, embroidery is used to give the illusion of traditional smocking. Purl-stitch guides make placing the embroidery a breeze. Our version is designed for a baby boy, but it would be easy to reverse the button band for a little girl.

SIZES
3 (6, 9, 12, 18, 24) months

FINISHED MEASUREMENTS
19 (20½, 23¼, 24¾, 27, 30)" chest, buttoned

YARN
Berroco Comfort Chunky (50% super fine nylon / 50% super fine acrylic; 100 grams /150 yards): 2 (2, 2, 3, 3, 3) skeins #5707 Boy Blue (MC); 1 skein #5716 Chambray (A)

NEEDLES
One pair straight needles size US 10½ (6.5 mm)
Change needle size if necessary to obtain correct gauge.

NOTIONS
Five ½" buttons; stitch holders; tapestry needle

GAUGE
14 sts and 20 rows = 4" (10 cm) in Stockinette stitch (St st)

STITCH PATTERN
1X1 RIB (odd number of sts; 1-row repeat)
Row 1 (RS): K1, *p1, k1; repeat from * to end.
Row 2: Knit the knit sts and purl the purl sts as they face you. Repeat Row 2 for 1x1 Rib.

BODY
Note: Body is worked in one piece back and forth to armholes.
Using MC, CO 73 (79, 87, 93, 101, 111) sts. Begin 1x1 Rib; work even for 6 rows.
Next Row (RS): Work 5 sts and transfer to st holder, k3 (2, 2, 1, 1, 2), work Row 1 of Chart to last 8 (7, 7, 6, 6, 7) sts, k3 (2, 2, 1, 1, 2), transfer remaining 5 sts to st holder—63 (69, 77, 83, 91, 101) sts remain. Work Rows 2-8 of Chart once, then Rows 1-9 once.
Next Row (WS): Change to St st; work even until piece measures 5½ (5½, 6, 6, 6¾, 6¾)" from the beginning, ending with a WS row.
Divide for Fronts and Back (RS): Work 14 (16, 18, 20, 22, 25) sts and transfer to st holder for Right Front, work 35 (37, 41, 43, 47, 51) sts for Back, transfer next 14 (16, 18, 20, 22, 25) sts to st holder for Left Front.

BACK
Next Row (WS): Work even until armholes measure 4½ (4½, 5, 5, 5¼, 5¼)". BO all sts.

LEFT FRONT

Next Row (RS): With RS facing, rejoin yarn to sts on holder for Left Front; continuing in St st, work even until armhole measures 3 (3, 3½, 3½, 3¾, 3¾)", ending with a RS row.

SHAPE NECK
Next Row (WS): BO 2 (4, 4, 4, 3, 4) sts at neck edge once, 2 (2, 3, 2, 3, 4) sts once, then 0 (0, 0, 2, 3, 3) sts once—10 (10, 11, 12, 13, 14) sts remain. Work even until armhole measures same as for Back. BO all sts.

RIGHT FRONT

Next Row (WS): With WS facing, rejoin yarn to sts on holder for Right Front. Work as for Left Front, reversing all shaping.

SLEEVE

Using MC, CO 17 (17, 19, 19, 21, 21) sts. Begin 1x1 Rib; work even for 6 rows. Change to St st; work even for 2 rows.

SHAPE SLEEVE
Next Row (RS): Increase 1 st each side this row, every 4 rows 5 (5, 4, 4, 4, 4) times, then every other row 1 (1, 3, 3, 3, 3) time(s), as follows: K1, M1, work to last st, M1, k1—31 (31, 35, 35, 37, 37) sts. Work even until piece measures 6½" from the beginning, ending with a WS row. BO all sts.

FINISHING

Sew shoulder seams. Sew in Sleeves. Sew Sleeve seams.

Neckband: With RS facing, using MC, pick up and knit 10 (10, 12, 12, 13, 14) sts along Right Front neck edge, 17 (19, 21, 21, 23, 25) sts along Back neck, and 10 (10, 12, 12, 13, 14) sts along Left Front neck edge—37 (39, 45, 45, 49, 53) sts. Begin 1x1 Rib; work even for 4 rows. BO all sts in pattern.

Button Band: With WS facing, CO 1 st, work across sts on hold for Right Front—6 sts.
Next Row (RS): Work to last st, k1 (edge st, keep in St st). Work even until Band, slightly stretched, reaches top of Neckband. BO all sts in pattern. Sew Band in place. Place markers for buttons, the first just below Neckband, the last just above end of bottom ribbing, and 3 more evenly spaced between.

Buttonhole Band: With RS facing, CO 1 st, work across sts on hold for Left Front—6 sts.
Next Row (WS): Work to last st, p1 (edge st, keep in St st).
Buttonhole Row (RS): Work 2 sts, yo, k2tog, work 2 sts. Work even, working buttonholes opposite markers, until Band, slightly stretched, reaches top of Neckband. BO all sts in pattern. Sew Band in place. Sew buttons opposite buttonholes.

Embroidery: Using tapestry needle and A, work embroidery pattern from Embroidery Chart, making sure not to weave yarn too tightly.

EMBROIDERY CHART

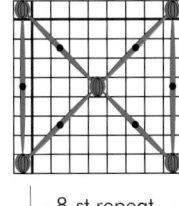

└─ 8-st repeat ─┘

CHART

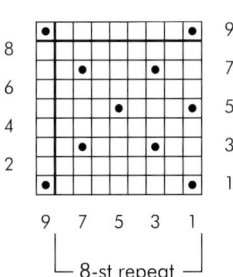

└─ 8-st repeat ─┘

KEY

☐ Knit stitch   ◉ Wrap purl st 5 times loosely.

⊡ Purl stitch   ⊞ Weave yarn under purl st.

KEY

☐ Knit on RS, purl on WS.

⊡ Purl on RS, knit on WS.

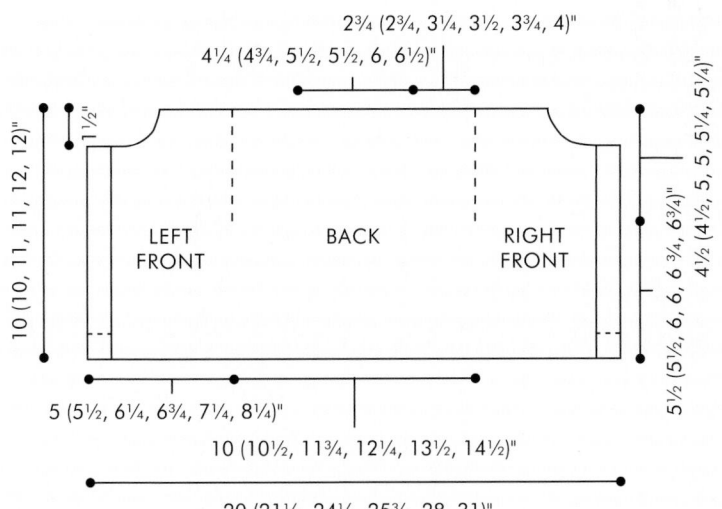

2¾ (2¾, 3¼, 3½, 3¾, 4)"

4¼ (4¾, 5½, 5½, 6, 6½)"

1½"

10 (10, 11, 11, 12, 12)"

LEFT FRONT   BACK   RIGHT FRONT

4½ (4½, 5, 5, 5¼, 5¼)"

5½ (5½, 6, 6, 6¾, 6¾)"

5 (5½, 6¼, 6¾, 7¼, 8¼)"

10 (10½, 11¾, 12¼, 13½, 14½)"

20 (21½, 24¼, 25¾, 28, 31)"

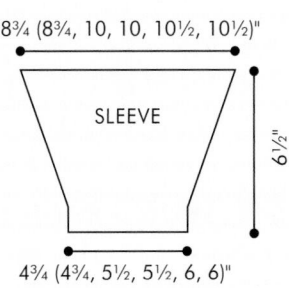

8¾ (8¾, 10, 10, 10½, 10½)"

SLEEVE

6½"

4¾ (4¾, 5½, 5½, 6, 6)"

Battenberg Blanket

The stitch used for this blanket has the appearance of complicated waves, but it's really just an easy ribbing that starts one stitch to the right every few rows. For an unusual touch, the edging is worked along the sides, but doesn't meet in the corners.

FINISHED MEASUREMENTS
35" wide x 42" long

YARN
Berroco Vintage (50% acrylic / 40% wool / 10% nylon; 100 grams / 217 yards): 6 hanks #5101 Mochi (MC); 1 hank #5102 Butter-cream (A)

NEEDLES
One pair straight needles size US 8 (5 mm)
Change needle size if necessary to obtain correct gauge.

GAUGE
18 sts and 24 rows = 4" (10 cm) in Shifting Ribs

STITCH PATTERN
SHIFTING RIBS (multiple of 6 sts + 4; 12-row repeat)
Rows 1 and 3 (RS): *K4, p2; repeat from * to last 4 sts, k4.
Rows 2 and 4: *P4, k2; repeat from * to last 4 sts, p4.
Rows 5 and 7: K2, *p2, k4; repeat from * to last 2 sts, p2.
Rows 6 and 8: *K2, p4; repeat from * to last 4 sts, k2, p2.
Rows 9 and 11: *P2, k4; repeat from * to last 4 sts, p2, k2.
Rows 10 and 12: P2, *k2, p4; repeat from * to last 2 sts, k2.
Repeat Rows 1-12 for Shifting Ribs.

BLANKET
Using MC, CO 148 sts. Begin Shifting Ribs; work even until piece measures 40" from the beginning, ending with a RS row.
Next Row (WS): Change to A; knit 12 rows. BO all sts knitwise.

FINISHING
Bottom Edging: With RS facing, using A, pick up and knit 148 sts along CO edge. Knit 12 rows. BO all sts knitwise.

Side Edging: With RS facing, using A, pick up and knit 175 sts along one long side edge of Blanket. Knit 12 rows. BO all sts knitwise. Repeat for opposite edge.

Block lightly (see Special Techniques, page 156).

Pink
Lemonade
Dress

This simple A-line shift is embellished with a column of openwork medallions, much like pretty citrus slices floating in a glass of pink lemonade. The "slices" are attached with a line of chain stitch, while coordinating buttons add detail and dimension.

SIZES
3 (6, 9, 12, 18, 24) months

FINISHED MEASUREMENTS
18 (19, 21, 22½, 25½, 27)" chest

YARN
Berroco Comfort (50% super fine nylon / 50% super fine acrylic; 100 grams / 210 yards): 2 (2, 2, 2, 3, 3) skeins #9704 Peach (MC); 1 skein each #9706 Limone (A) and #9702 Pearl (B)

CROCHET HOOKS
One crochet hook size US I/9 (5.5 mm)
One crochet hook size US H/8 (5 mm)
Change hook size if necessary to obtain correct gauge

NOTIONS
Four 1" buttons

GAUGE
18 sts and 17 rows = 4" (10 cm) in Open Single Crochet (Open sc), using larger hook

STITCH PATTERN
OPEN SINGLE CROCHET (odd number of sts + 1 ch; 1-row repeat)
Set-Up Row: Sc in second ch from hook, *ch 1, skip next ch, sc in next ch; repeat from * to end, turn.
All Rows: Ch 1, sc in first sc, *ch 1, skip ch-1 sp, sc in next sc; repeat from * to end, turn.

BACK
Using smaller crochet hook and MC, ch 58 (60, 64, 68, 74, 78). Begin Open sc; work even for 9 rows—57 (59, 63, 67, 73, 77) sts remain.

SHAPE SIDES
Decrease Row: Ch 1, pull a loop through first sc, next ch and next sc, yo and pull through 3 loops on hook (2 decreases), work to end—55 (57, 61, 65, 71, 75) sts remain.
Repeat Decrease Row once—53 (55, 59, 63, 69, 73) sts remain. *Work even for 9 rows. Repeat Decrease Row twice. Repeat from * twice—41 (43, 47, 51, 57, 61) sts. Work even until piece measures 11".

SHAPE ARMHOLES

Next Row: Slip st into first 4 (4, 4, 6, 6) sts, work to last 4 (4, 4, 4, 6, 6) sts, turn.

Decrease Row: Ch 1, pull a loop through first sc, next ch and next sc, yo and pull through 3 loops on hook (2 decreases), work to end—31 (33, 37, 41, 43, 47) sts remain. Repeat Decrease Row 1 (1, 3, 3, 3, 5) time(s)—29 (31, 31, 35, 37, 37) sts remain. Work even until armhole measures 3½ (3¾, 4, 4½, 5, 5½)". Fasten off.

FRONT

Work as for Back until armhole measures 2 (2¼, 2½, 3, 3½, 4)".

SHAPE NECK

Next Row: Work 7 (8, 8, 10, 11, 11) sts, skip center 15 sts, join a second ball of yarn to last 7 (8, 8, 10, 11, 11) sts, work to end. Working both sides at the same time, work Decrease Row at each neck edge once—5 (6, 6, 8, 9, 9) sts remain each side. Work even until armhole measures 3½ (3¾, 4, 4½, 5, 5½)". Fasten off.

FINISHING

Sew shoulder seams. Sew side seams.

CIRCLE (make 4)

Using larger hook and A, begin with a sliding loop.

Rnd 1: Ch 3 (counts as dc), work 11 dc in ring, join with a slip st in top of ch 3.

Rnd 2: Ch 4 (counts as dc and ch 1), *dc in next dc, ch 1; repeat from * to end, slip st in third ch of beginning ch 4.

Rnd 3: Ch 1, sc in same st, ch 3, *sc in next dc, ch 3; repeat from * to end, slip st in first sc. Fasten off.

Rnd 4: Using B, join with a slip st in any ch-3 sp, *5 sc in ch-3 sp; repeat from * to end, slip st in first sc. Fasten off. Pin Circles to center Front, evenly sp from top of neckline to bottom edge. Attach with a chain st through centers of Circles, beginning with bottom Circle. Sew button to center of each Circle.

Neck Edging: Using smaller hook and MC, work 1 rnd Rev sc evenly around neck opening.

Armhole Edging: Using smaller hook and MC, work 1 rnd Rev sc evenly around each armhole edge.

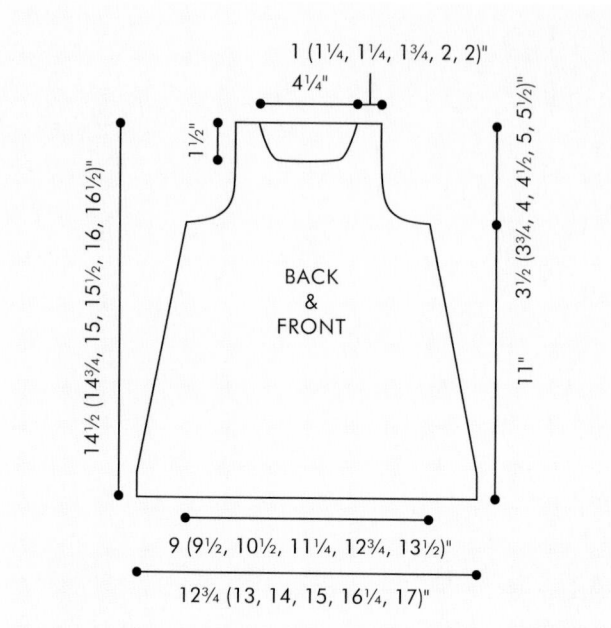

Kumquat Blanket

In China, the kumquat is believed to bring good luck, so perhaps this blanket will bring your little one a bit of good luck, too! Each "kumquat" is made from eight wedges of color, and five kumquats in an off-center row are set against a vibrant yellow background.

FINISHED MEASUREMENTS
38" wide x 42" long

YARN
Berroco Vintage (50% acrylic / 40% wool / 10% nylon; 100 grams / 217 yards): 5 hanks #5122 Banane (MC); 1 hank each #5164 Tang (A), #51179 Apricot (B), #51180 Grapefruit (C), #5123 Blush (D), and #5166 Sakura (E)

NEEDLES
One pair straight needles size US 8 (5 mm)
Change needle size if necessary to obtain correct gauge.

NOTIONS
Stitch markers

GAUGE
18 sts and 24 rows = 4" (10 cm) in Stockinette stitch (St st)

LEFT SIDE

Using MC, CO 42 sts. Begin St st; purl 1 row.

SHAPE LEFT SIDE

***Decrease Row 1 (RS):** BO 2 sts at beginning of this row, then every other row twice—36 sts remain. Purl 1 row.

Decrease Row 2 (RS): BO 1 st at beginning of this row, then every other row 3 times—32 sts remain. Work even for 21 rows.

Increase Row 1 (RS): CO 1 st at beginning of this row, then every other row 3 times—36 sts. Purl 1 row.

Increase Row 2 (RS): CO 2 sts at beginning of this row, then every other row twice—42 sts. Purl 1 row. Repeat from * 4 times. BO all sts.

RIGHT SIDE

Using MC, CO 104 sts. Work as for Left Side, reversing all shaping, working decreases and increases at beginning of WS rows instead of at beginning of RS rows.

OCTAGONS 1 AND 5

Using A, CO 16 sts, pm, using E, CO 15 sts, pm, using B, CO 15 sts, pm, using C, CO 15 sts, pm, using A, CO 15 sts, pm, using D, CO 15 sts, pm, using B, CO 15 sts, pm, using C, CO 16 sts—122 sts. Working in colors as established, begin St st; purl 1 row.

SHAPE OCTAGON

Decrease Row (RS): Decrease 16 sts this row, every 4 rows 4 times, then every other row twice, as follows: K1, [ssk, knit to 2 sts before marker, k2tog] 8 times, k1—10 sts remain. Cut yarn, leaving an 8" tail, thread though remaining sts, pull tight, and fasten off. Sew side edges to form an Octagon.

OCTAGON 2

Using C, CO 16 sts, pm, using D, CO 15 sts, pm, using A, CO 15 sts, pm, using E, CO 15 sts, pm, using B, CO 15 sts, pm, using D, CO 15 sts, pm, using A, CO 15 sts, pm, using E, CO 16 sts—122 sts. Complete as for Octagon 1.

OCTAGON 3

Using D, CO 16 sts, pm, using C, CO 15 sts, pm, using A, CO 15 sts, pm, using E, CO 15 sts, pm, using D, CO 15 sts, pm, using C, CO 15 sts, pm, using B, CO 15 sts, pm, using E, CO 16 sts—122 sts. Complete as for Octagon 1.

OCTAGON 4

Using B, CO 16 sts, pm, using D, CO 15 sts, pm, using C, CO 15 sts, pm, using A, CO 15 sts, pm, using B, CO 15 sts, pm, using E, CO 15 sts, pm, using C, CO 15 sts, pm, using A, CO 16 sts—122 sts. Complete as for Octagon 1.

ASSEMBLY DIAGRAM

KEY — MC A B C D E

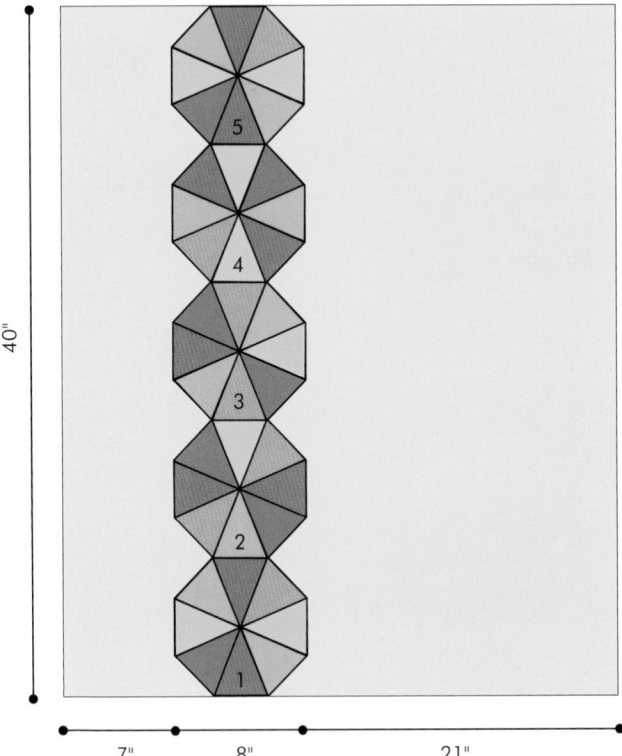

FINISHING

Sew Octagons together according to Assembly Diagram. Sew Right and Left Sides to Octagons according to Assembly Diagram.

Side Edging: With RS facing, using C, pick up and knit 180 sts evenly along one long side edge. Knit 2 rows. Change to B; knit 2 rows. Change to C; knit 2 rows. Change to B; knit 1 row. BO all sts. Repeat for opposite side edge.

Top and Bottom Edging: With RS facing, using C, pick up and knit 165 sts evenly along bottom edge, including Side Edging. Work as for Side Edging. Repeat for top edge.

Block lightly (see Special Techniques, page 156).

Campus
Onesie

A quirky combination of green stripes lends a modern touch to this wardrobe staple. The lap shoulder neckline and a snapped crotch make it easy to put on and take off. (Well, as easy as possible anyway!)

SIZES
3 (6, 9, 12) months

FINISHED MEASUREMENTS
18 (19, 19½, 22)" chest

YARN
Berroco Comfort DK (50% super fine nylon / 50% super fine acrylic; 50 grams / 178 yards): 1 (1, 2, 2) skein(s) each #2719 Sunshine (A) and #2761 Lovage (B); 1 skein #2709 Menthe (C)

NEEDLES
One pair straight needles size US 7 (4.5 mm)
One pair straight needles size US 5 (3.75 mm)
Change needle size if necessary to obtain correct gauge.

NOTIONS
Stitch markers; 3 medium snaps

GAUGE
22 sts and 32 rows = 4" (10 cm) in Stockinette stitch (St st), using larger needles

STITCH PATTERNS
1X1 RIB (odd number of sts; 1-row repeat)
Row 1 (RS): K1 *p1, k1; repeat from * to end.
Row 2: Knit the knit sts and purl the purl sts as they face you. Repeat Row 2 for 1x1 Rib.

STRIPE SEQUENCE
Working in St st, work *2 rows A, then 2 rows B; repeat from * for Stripe Sequence.

BACK
Using larger needles and A, CO 14 sts for crotch. Purl 1 row. Begin Stripe Sequence.

SHAPE LEG OPENINGS
Next Row (RS): Increase 1 st each side this row, then every other row 14 (15, 16, 19) times, as follows: K1, M1, work to last st, M1, k1—44 (46, 48, 54) sts. Purl 1 row.
Next Row (RS): CO 3 sts at beginning of next 2 rows—50 (52, 54, 60) sts. Work even until piece measures 13 (13¼, 13½, 14¼)" from the beginning, ending with a WS row. Place markers each side for armhole. Work even until armhole measures 3½ (3¾, 4, 4¼)" from marker, ending with a WS row. Place markers each side for upper armhole seams.

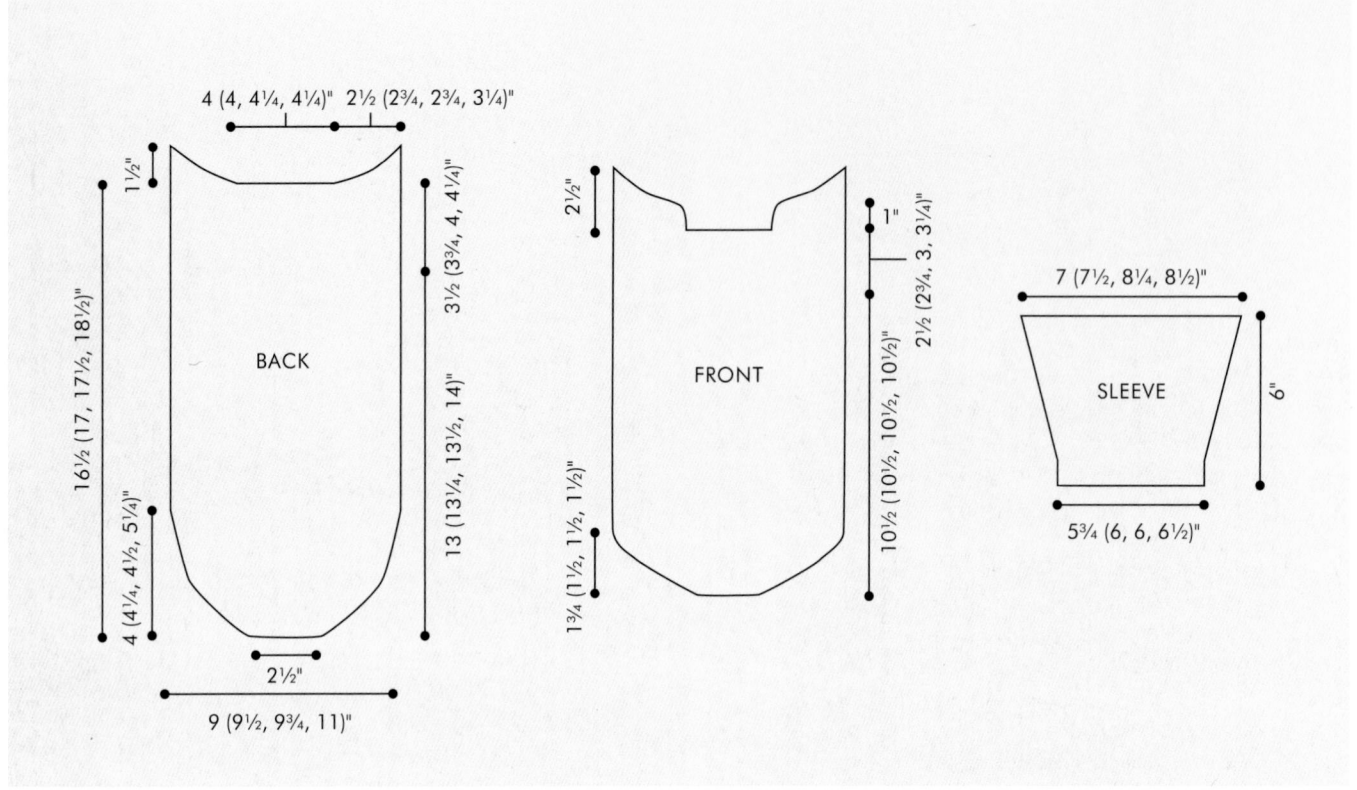

SHAPE NECK AND SHOULDERS

Next Row (RS): K14 (15, 15, 18), join a second ball of yarn and BO center 22 (22, 24, 24) sts, knit to end. Working both sides at the same time, BO 2 (2, 2, 3) sts at each neck edge 4 (3, 3, 6) times, then 3 (3, 3, 0) sts 2 (3, 3, 0) times.

FRONT

Using larger needles and A, CO 14 sts for crotch. Purl 1 row. Begin Stripe Sequence.

SHAPE FRONT

Next Row (RS): CO 3 (3, 3, 4) sts at beginning of next 12 (10, 10, 10) rows, then 0 (4, 5, 3) sts at beginning of next 2 rows—50 (52, 54, 60) sts. Work even until piece measures 10½" from the beginning, ending with a WS row. Place markers each side for armholes. Work even until piece measures 13 (13¼, 13½, 13¾)" from the beginning, ending with a WS row.

SHAPE NECK

Next Row (RS): K14 (15, 15, 18), join a second ball of yarn and BO center 22 (22, 24, 24) sts, knit to end. Working both sides at the same time, work even for 7 rows. Place markers each side for upper armhole seams.

SHAPE SHOULDERS

Next Row (RS): BO 2 (2, 2, 3) sts at each neck edge 4 (3, 3, 6) times, then 3 (3, 3, 0) sts 2 (3, 3, 0) times.

SLEEVES

Using smaller needles and C, CO 39 (41, 41, 43) sts. Begin 1x1 Rib; work even for 1", decreasing 8 sts evenly on last WS row—31 (33, 33, 35) sts remain.
Next Row (RS): Change to larger needles and A. Begin Stripe Sequence; work even for 6 rows.

SHAPE SLEEVE

Next Row (RS): Increase 1 st each side this row, every 8 (8, 6, 6) rows 3 (3, 4, 4) times, then every 4 rows 0 (0, 1, 1) time(s), as follows: K1, M1, work to last st, M1, k1—39 (41, 45, 47) sts. Work even until piece measures 6" from the beginning. BO all sts.

FINISHING

Front Leg/Crotch Band: With RS facing, using smaller needles and C, and beginning at top of right leg opening, pick up and knit 26 (28, 28, 30) sts along right leg shaping edge, pm, 1 st in corner, 11 sts along CO edge, pm, 1 st in corner, then 26 (28, 28, 30) sts along left leg shaping edge—65 (69, 69, 73) sts. Begin 1x1 Rib; work even for 1 row.

Next Row (RS): Increase 4 sts this row, then every other row once, as follows: [Work to marker, M1, sm, k1, M1] twice, work to end—73 (77, 77, 81) sts. BO sll sts in pattern.

Back Leg/Crotch Band: With RS facing, using smaller needles and C, and beginning at top of left leg opening, pick up and knit 36 (38, 38, 40) sts along left leg shaping edge, pm, 1 st in corner, 11 sts along CO edge, pm, 1 st in corner, then 36 (38, 38, 40) sts along right leg shaping edge—85 (89, 89, 93) sts. Complete as for Front Leg/Crotch Band—93 (97, 97, 101) sts. BO all sts in pattern.

Back Neck/Shoulder Band: With RS facing, using smaller needles and C, pick up and knit 18 (20, 20, 22) sts along right shoulder, pm, 1 st in corner, 23 (23, 25, 25) sts along Back neck, pm, 1 st in corner, then 18 (20, 20, 22) sts along left shoulder—61 (65, 67, 71) sts. Begin 1x1 Rib; work even for 1 row.

Next Row (RS): Decrease 4 sts this row, then every other row once, as follows: [Work to 2 sts before marker, ssk, sm, k1, k2tog] twice, work to end—53 (57, 59, 63) sts remain. BO all sts in pattern.

Front Neck/Shoulder Band: With RS facing, using smaller needles and C, pick up and knit 26 (28, 28, 30) sts along left shoulder, pm, 1 st in corner, 23 (23, 25, 25) sts along Front neck, pm, 1 st in corner, then 26 (28, 28, 30) sts along right shoulder—77 (81, 83, 87) sts. Complete as for Back Neck/Shoulder Band—69 (73, 75, 79) sts remain.

With RS of Front and Back facing, overlap Back shoulders over Front shoulders so that tips of Back shoulders meet Front upper armhole markers, and tips of Front shoulders meet Back upper armhole markers. Sew side edges between markers, making sure that Back is on top of Front. Sew in Sleeves. Sew side seams, ending at beginning of Leg/Crotch Bands. Sew Sleeve seams. Sew 3 snaps to back and front crotch opening.

Pomelo
Slice

Our cuddly citrus slice is a whimsical toy for baby, and it's just the right size for a small hand to grab on to. For a toddler, you might want to make six and add snaps, so the fruit can be assembled (and disassembled) over and over again.

FINISHED MEASUREMENTS
Approximately 3" wide x 7" long

YARN
Berroco Vintage (50% acrylic / 40% wool / 10% nylon; 100 grams / 217 yards): 1 hank each #51179 Apricot (A), #5111 Limone (B), and #51180 Grapefruit (C)

NEEDLES
One pair straight needles size US 7 (4.5 mm)
Change needle size if necessary to obtain correct gauge.

GAUGE
18 sts and 24 rows = 4" (10 cm) in Stockinette stitch (St st)

NOTIONS
Stuffing

CITRUS WEDGE
PEEL
Using A, CO 3 sts.
Increase Row 1 (RS): [K1-f/b] twice, k1—5 sts. Purl 1 row.
Increase Row 2: Increase 1 st each side this row, every other row once, then every 4 rows 5 times, as follows: K2, M1, knit to last 2 sts, M1, k2—19 sts. Work even for 3 rows.
Decrease Row 1 (RS): Decrease 1 st each side this row, then every 4 rows 5 times, as follows: K2, k2tog, knit to last 4 sts, ssk, k2—7 sts remain. Purl 1 row.

Decrease Row 2: K1, k2tog, k1, ssk, k1—5 sts remains. Purl 1 row.
Decrease Row 3: K2tog, k1, ssk—3 sts remains. BO all sts.

SIDE
With RS facing, using B, pick up and knit 35 sts along one side edge of Peel.
Rows 1 and 3 (WS): Knit.
Row 2: Purl.
Row 4: Change to C. Knit.
Rows 5 and 7: K5, *p1, k7; repeat from * to last 6 sts, p1, k5.
Row 6: Knit the knit sts and purl the purl sts as they face you.
Row 8: P2, p2tog, *k2tog, [p2tog] 3 times; repeat from * to last 7 sts, k2tog, [p2tog] twice, p1—19 sts remain.
Rows 9-13: Repeat Row 6.
Row 14: P2, *k2tog, p2tog; repeat from * to last st, p1—
11 sts remain.
Row 15: Repeat Row 6.
Row 16: P1, *k2tog; repeat from * to last 2 sts, p2tog—
6 sts remain.
Cut yarn, leaving an 8" tail, thread through remaining sts, pull tight, and fasten off. Repeat for second side of Peel.

FINISHING
Sew top seam, stuffing Wedge when seam is nearly complete. Sew remaining portion of seam.

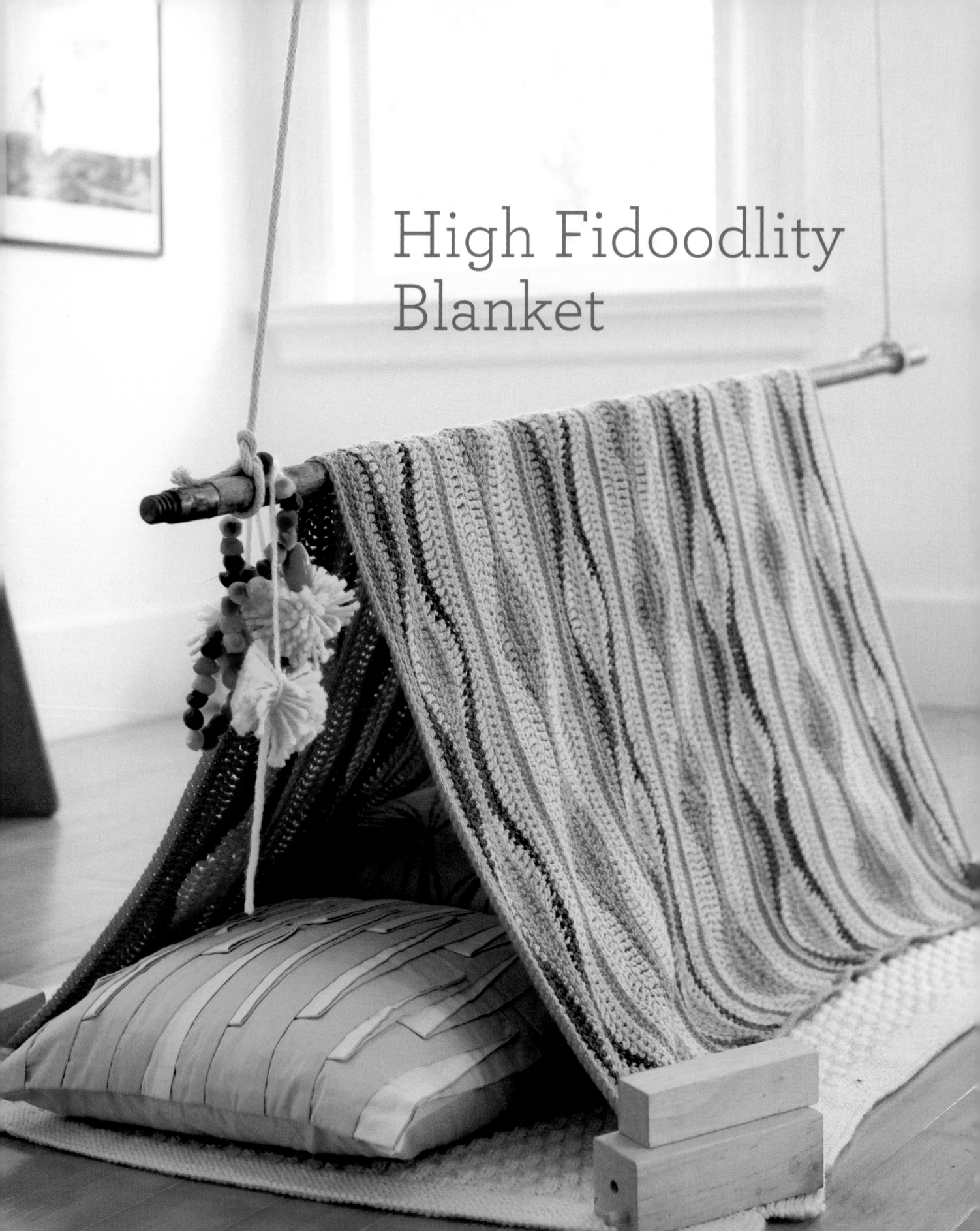

High Fidoodlity
Blanket

In the sixties, when I was growing up, my dad reveled in broad-casting tunes from his record collection throughout the house. "High fidelity" was a term proudly displayed on LPs at the time, and I have fond memories of Dad teasingly calling it "high fidoodlity." This blanket reminds me of artwork on albums from that era, and I like to think of it as an artistic impression of sound waves.

FINISHED MEASUREMENTS
38" wide x 46" long

YARN
Berroco Vintage (50% acrylic / 40% wool / 10% nylon; 100 grams / 217 yards): 2 hanks each #51180 Grapefruit (A), #5104 Mushroom (B), #5125 Aquae (D), and #5121 Sunny (E); 1 hank #5107 Cracked Pepper (C)

CROCHET HOOKS
One crochet hook size US H/8 (5 mm)
Change hook size if necessary to obtain correct gauge.

GAUGE
16 sts and 20 rows = 4" (10 cm) in Single Crochet (sc)

BLANKET

STRIP 1 (make 4)
Using A, ch 169.
Row 1 (RS): Sc in second ch from hook and in next 4 ch, *dc in next 4 ch, tr in next 6 ch, dc in next 4 ch, sc in next 10 ch**; repeat from * 5 times, dc in next 4 ch, tr in next 6 ch, dc in next 4 ch, sc in last 5 ch. Do not turn. Working along the other side of foundation ch, sc in first 5 ch, repeat from * to ** 6 times, dc in next 4 ch, tr in next 6 ch, dc in next 4 ch, sc in last 5 ch, turn—168 sts.
Row 2: Change to B, ch 1, *sc in next 5 sc, dc in next 4 dc, tr in next 6 tr, dc in next 4 dc, sc in next 10 sc **; repeat from * 5 times, dc in next 4 dc, tr in next 6 tr, dc in next 4 dc, sc in next 5 sc. Do not turn. Work 2 slip sts in end of Row 1. Working along other side of Row 1, repeat from * to ** 6 times, dc in next 4 dc, tr in next 6 tr, dc in next 4 dc, sc in last 5 dc, turn.

Row 3: Change to C, ch 3 (counts as 1 tr), tr in next 4 sc, *dc in next 4 dc, sc in next 6 sts, dc in next 4 dc, tr in next 10 sts; repeat from * 5 times, dc in next 4 dc, sc in next 6 tr, dc in next 4 dc, tr in last 5 sc, turn.
Row 4: Change to D, repeat Row 3.
Row 5: Ch 2 (counts as 1 dc), dc in next st and in each st to end, turn.
Row 6: Ch 1 (counts as 1 sc), sc in next dc and in each dc to end. Fasten off.
With RS facing, join C to other side of Row 2 with a slip st; repeat Row 3. Change to E; repeat Rows 4-6. Fasten off.

STRIP 2 (make 3)
Work as for Strip 1 in the following colors: Work Row 1 using D, Row 2 using A, and Rows 3-6 using B. With RS facing, join E to other side of Row 2 with a slip st; repeat Rows 3-6. Fasten off.

FINISHING
With RSs facing and D side of Strip 1 and E side of Strip 2 together, join A with slip st in first sc of Strip 1. *Insert hook into first sc of Strip 1 and first sc of Strip 2 and sc these 2 sts together. Repeat from * until all scs are joined. Fasten off. Continue to join Strips in this manner, alternating Strip 1 and Strip 2, until all 7 Strips are joined.

EDGING
Rnd 1: With RS facing, join A with a slip st in any corner of Blanket. Work 1 rnd sc around entire Blanket, join with a slip st in first sc.
Rnd 2: Ch 1, sc in each sc around, working 3 sc in each corner, join with a slip st in first sc. Fasten off.

Block lightly (see Special Techniques, page 156).

Compass
Cap

Twisted ribbing and sinuous round cables create bold graphic elements in this cap, making it modern and traditional at the same time. (You'll recognize the ogee-shaped cable from the edge of the Solaria Blanket on page 71.) Since the hat is worked in the round, there are no seams to bother baby.

SIZE
12-18 months

FINISHED MEASUREMENTS
15¼" circumference

YARN
Berroco Comfort (50% super fine nylon / 50% super fine acrylic; 100 grams / 210 yards): 1 skein #9764 Lidfors

NEEDLES
One 16" (40 cm) long circular (circ) needle size US 6 (4 mm)
One 16" (40 cm) long circular needle size US 4 (3.5 mm)
One set of five double-pointed needles (dpn) size US 6 (4 mm)
Change needle size if necessary to obtain correct gauge.

NOTIONS
Stitch markers; cable needle (cn)

GAUGE
22 sts and 32 rows = 4" (10 cm) in Cable Pattern from Chart, using larger needle

STITCH PATTERN
2X2 RIB (multiple of 4 sts; 1-rnd repeat)
All Rnds: *K2, p2; repeat from * to end.

HAT
Using smaller circ needle, CO 84 sts. Join for working in the rnd, being careful not to twist sts; pm for beginning of rnd. Begin 2x2 Rib; work even for ½". Change to larger needle. Knit 1 rnd. Purl 1 rnd. Knit 1 rnd.
Next Rnd: *Work Cable Pattern from Chart over 21 sts, pm; repeat from * to end, omitting pm on final repeat. Work even until Chart has been completed, working decreases as indicated in Chart—12 sts remain. *Note: Change to dpns when necessary for number of sts on needle.* Cut yarn, leaving an 8" tail; thread tail through remaining sts, pull tight, and fasten off.

KEY

☐	Knit
⊡	Purl
⧄	K1-tbl
⊠	K2tog
⊠	Ssk
⊠	P2tog
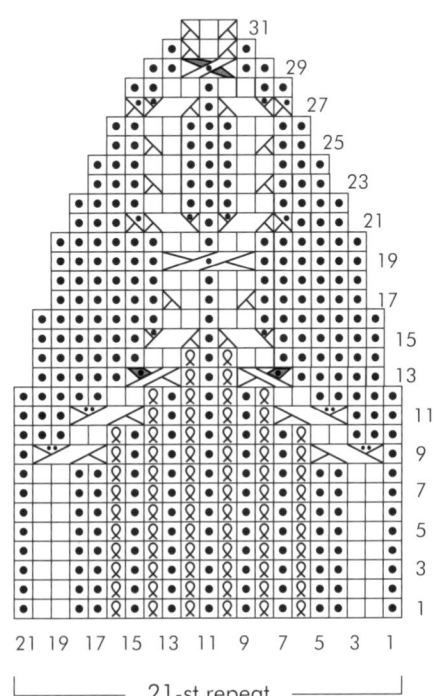	Slip 2 sts to cn and hold to front, p1, k2 from cn.
	Slip 1 st to cn and hold to back, k2, p1 from cn.

	Slip 2 sts to cn and hold to front, p2tog, k2 from cn.
	Slip 2 sts to cn and hold to back, k2, p2tog from cn.
	Slip 3 sts to cn and hold to back, k2tog, (p1, k2tog) from cn.
	Slip 2 sts to cn and hold to front, p2, k2 from cn.
	Slip 2 sts to cn and hold to back, k2, p2 from cn.
	Slip 3 sts to cn and hold to back, k2, (p1, k2) from cn.

CABLE PATTERN

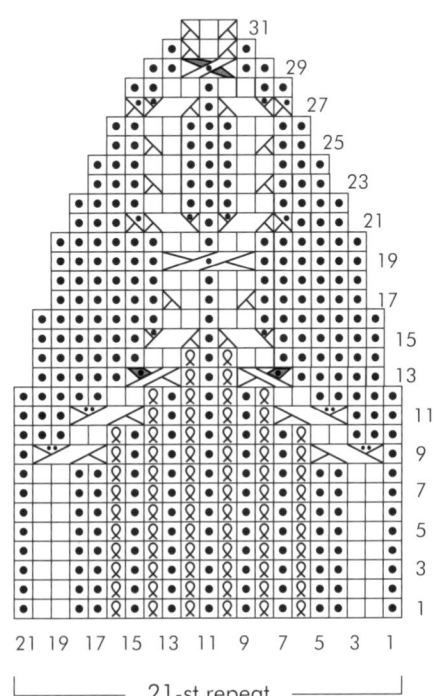

31
29
27
25
23
21
19
17
15
13
11
9
7
5
3
1

21 19 17 15 13 11 9 7 5 3 1

└─── 21-st repeat ───┘

Citrus Grove Blanket

In colors inspired by citrus groves all over the world, this blanket combines easy crochet stitches into a patchwork of colorful rectangles. It is worked in strips and sewn up at the end, so you won't have to tote around the whole project as you work.

FINISHED MEASUREMENTS
36" wide x 44" long

YARN
Berroco Comfort (50% super fine nylon / 50% super fine acrylic; 100 grams / 210 yards): 2 skeins each #9740 Seedling (A), #9704 Peach (B), #9732 Primary Yellow (C), #9724 Pumpkin (D), #9791 Gooseberry Heather (E), #9764 Lidfors (F), and #9706 Limone (G)

CROCHET HOOKS
One crochet hook size US I/9 (5.5 mm)
One crochet hook size US H/8 (5 mm)
Change hook size if necessary to obtain correct gauge.

GAUGE
14 sts and 18 rows = 4" (10 cm) in Single Crochet (sc), using larger hook

STRIP 1
Using larger hook and A, ch 22. Begin sc; work even until piece measures 6" from the beginning—21 sc.
Next Row: Change to smaller hook and B; ch 2, dc in each sc to end. Continuing in dc, work even for 8".
Next Row: Change to larger hook and C; ch 1, sc-tbl in each dc to end. Continuing in sc-tbl, work even for 4".

Next Row: Change to D; ch 1, sc in each sc-tbl to end. Continuing in sc, work even for 6".

Next Row: Change to smaller hook and E; ch 2, dc in each sc to end. Continuing in dc, work even for 8".

Next Row: Change to larger hook and F; ch 1, sc-tbl in each dc to end. Continuing in sc-tbl, work even for 8".

Next Row: Change to smaller hook and G; ch 2, dc-tbl in each sc-tbl to end. Continuing in dc-tbl, work even for 4". Fasten off.

STRIP 2

Using larger hook and C, ch 22. Sc in second ch from hook and in each ch to end, turn—21 sc.

Next Row: Begin sc-tbl; work even until piece measures 8" from the beginning.

Next Row: Change to D; ch 1, sc in each sc-tbl to end. Continuing in sc, work even for 4".

Next Row: Change to smaller hook and E; ch 2, dc in each sc to end. Continuing in dc, work even for 8".

Next Row: Change to larger hook and F; ch 1, sc-tbl in each dc to end. Continuing in sc-tbl, work even for 8".

Next Row: Change to smaller hook and G; ch 2, dc-tbl in each sc-tbl to end. Continuing in dc-tbl, work even for 6".

Next Row: Change to smaller hook and B; ch 2, dc in each dc-tbl to end. Continuing in dc, work for 4".

Next Row: Change to larger hook and A; ch 1, sc in each dc to end. Continuing in sc, work even for 6". Fasten off.

STRIP 3

Using larger hook and F, ch 22. Sc in second ch from hook and in each ch to end, turn—21 sc.

Next Row: Begin sc-tbl; work even until piece measures 4" from the beginning.

Next Row: Change to A; ch 1, sc in each sc-tbl to end. Continuing in sc, work even for 8".

Next Row: Change to smaller hook and G; ch 2, dc-tbl in each sc to end. Continuing in dc-tbl, work even for 6".

Next Row: Change to B; ch 2, dc in each dc-tbl to end. Continuing in dc, work even for 8".

Next Row: Change to E; ch 2, dc in each dc to end. Continuing in dc, work even for 6".

Next Row: Change to larger hook and C; ch 1, sc-tbl in each dc to end. Continuing in sc-tbl, work even for 8".

Next Row: Change to D; ch 1, sc in each sc-tbl to end. Continuing in sc, work even for 4". Fasten off.

STRIP 4

Using larger hook and D, ch 22. Begin sc; work even until piece measures 8" from the beginning—21 sc.

Next Row: Change to smaller hook and B; ch 2, dc in each sc to end. Continuing in dc, work even for 6".

Next Row: Change to larger hook and C; ch 1, sc-tbl in each dc to end. Continuing in sc-tbl, work even for 4".

Next Row: Change to A; ch 1, sc in each sc-tbl to end. Continuing in sc, work even for 6".

Next Row: Change to smaller hook and G; ch 2, dc-tbl in each sc to end. Continuing in dc-tbl, work even for 8".

Next Row: Change to E; ch 2, dc in each dc-tbl to end. Continuing in dc, work even for 4".

Next Row: Change to larger hook and F; ch 1, sc-tbl in each dc to end. Continuing in sc-tbl, work even for 8". Fasten off.

STRIP 5

Using smaller hook and G; ch 22. Begin dc-tbl; work even until piece measures 4" from the beginning—21 dc-tbl.

Next Row: Change to larger hook and F; ch 1, sc-tbl in each dc-tbl to end. Continuing in sc-tbl, work even for 8".

Next Row: Change to smaller hook and E; ch 2, dc in each sc-tbl to end. Continuing in dc, work even for 8".

Next Row: Change to larger hook and D; ch 1, sc in each dc to end. Continuing in sc, work even for 6".

Next Row: Change to C; ch 1, sc-tbl in each sc to end. Continuing in sc-tbl, work even for 4".

Next Row: Change to smaller hook and B; ch 2, dc in each sc-tbl to end. Continuing in dc, work even for 8".

Next Row: Change to larger hook and A; ch 1, sc in each dc to end. Continuing in sc, work even for 6". Fasten off.

STRIP 6

Using larger hook and A, ch 22. Begin sc; work even until piece measures 6"—21 sc.

Next Row: Change to smaller hook and B; ch 2, dc in each sc to end. Continuing in dc, work even for 4".

Next Row: Change to G; ch 2, dc-tbl in each dc to end. Continuing in dc-tbl, work even for 8".

Next Row: Change to larger hook and F; ch 1, sc-tbl in each dc-tbl to end. Continuing in sc-tbl, work even for 6".

Next Row: Change to smaller hook and E; ch 2, dc in each sc-tbl to end. Continuing in dc, work even for 8".

Next Row: Change to larger hook and D; ch 1, sc in each dc to end. Continuing in sc, work even for 4".

Next Row: Change to C; ch 1, sc-tbl in each sc to end. Continuing in sc-tbl, work even for 8". Fasten off.

FINISHING

With top edges aligned, sew Strips together from right to left in the order they were worked.

Block lightly (see Special Techniques, page 156).

Bobbled Blanket

Eyelet increases divide this blanket into four quarters, each of which is finished with rows of oversized bobbles. Softly contrasting shades of off white and pale yellow are classic and timeless—a perfect choice when you don't know if your gift will be for a baby boy or a baby girl.

FINISHED MEASUREMENTS
46" wide x 46" long

YARN
Berroco Comfort (50% super fine nylon / 50% super fine acrylic; 100 grams / 210 yards): 5 skeins #9702 Pearl (A); 3 skeins #9701 Ivory (B)

NEEDLES
One pair straight needles size US 9 (5.5 mm)
Change needle size if necessary to obtain correct gauge.

GAUGE
18 sts and 24 rows = 4" (10 cm) in Broken Rib

ABBREVIATION
MB (Make Bobble): Knit into front, back, front, back, then front of next st to increase to 5 sts, [slip 5 sts back to left-hand needle and knit them] 5 times, slip 5 sts back to left-hand needle, k2tog, k1, k2tog, slip 3 sts back to left-hand needle, k3tog—1 st remains.

STITCH PATTERNS
BROKEN RIB (odd number of sts; 2-row repeat)
Row 1 (WS): P1, *k1, p1; repeat from * to end.
Row 2: Knit.
Repeat Rows 1 and 2 for Broken Rib.

3X3 RIB (multiple of 6 sts + 3; 1-row repeat)
Row 1 (RS): K3, *p3, k3; repeat from * to end.
Row 2: Knit the knit sts and purl the purl sts as they face you.
Repeat Row 2 for 3x3 Rib.

TRIANGLE (make 4)

Using A, CO 3 sts.

Row 1 (RS): K1, [yo, k1] twice—5 sts.

Row 2: Purl.

Row 3: K2, yo, k1, yo, k2—7 sts.

Row 4: K3, p1, k3.

Row 5: K2, yo, knit to last 2 sts, yo, k2—9 sts.

Row 6: K3, work Broken Rib to last 3 sts, k3.

Row 7: K2, yo, work to last 2 sts, yo, k2—11 sts.

Row 8: K2, work to last 2 sts, working increased sts into Broken Rib, k2.

Row 9: K2, yo, work to last 2 sts, yo, k2—13 sts.

Row 10: K3, work to last 3 sts, working increased sts into Broken Rib, k3.

Repeat Rows 7-10 twenty-six times—117 sts.

Decrease Row 1 (RS): Change to B; k2, ssk, *MB, k2; repeat from * to last 5 sts, MB, k2tog, k2—115 sts remain.

Next Row: K2, purl to last 2 sts, k2.

Decrease Row 2 (RS): K2, ssk, k2, *MB, k2; repeat from * to last 7 sts, MB, k2, k2tog, k2—113 sts remain.

Next Row: K2, purl to last 2 sts, k2.

Decrease Row 3: Change to A. Decrease 1 st each side this row, then every other row twice, as follows: K2, ssk, work in 3x3 Rib to last 4 sts, k2tog, k2—107 sts remain. Work even for 1 row.

Decrease Row 4: Change to B; k2, ssk, knit to last 4 sts, k2tog, k2—105 sts remain.

Next Row: Knit.

Decrease Row 5: Change to A. Decrease 1 st each side this row, then every other row once, as follows: K2, ssk, work in 3x3 Rib as previously established to last 4 sts, k2tog, k2—101 sts remain.

Next Row: K2, work to last 2 sts, k2.

Decrease Row 6: Change to B; k2, ssk, k1, *MB, k2; repeat from * to last 6 sts, MB, k1, k2tog, k2—99 sts remain.

Next Row: K2, purl to last 2 sts, k2.

Decrease Row 7: K2, ssk, k3, *MB, k2; repeat from * to last 8 sts, MB, k3, k2tog, k2—97 sts remain.

Next Row: K2, purl to last 2 sts, k2.

Decrease Row 8: Decrease 1 st each side this row then every other row once, as follows: K2, ssk, work in 3x3 Rib as previously established to last 4 sts, k2tog, k2—93 sts remain.

Next Row: K2, work to last 2 sts, k2. BO all sts in pattern.

FINISHING

Sew Triangles together, beginning at center, and sewing through first bobble row.

Block lightly (see Special Techniques, page 156).

Abigail
Bolero

Ruffles along its edges give this cute bolero the romantic feel of bygone eras. Perhaps a young Abigail Adams wore a similar style to keep herself warm in the evening.

SIZES
3 (6, 9, 12, 18, 24) months

FINISHED MEASUREMENTS
19 (20½, 23, 24½, 26, 30)" chest

YARN
Berroco Vintage (50% acrylic / 40% wool / 10% nylon; 100 grams / 217 yards): 1 (2, 2, 2, 2, 3) hank(s) #5111 Limone (MC); 1 hank #5104 Mushroom (A)

CROCHET HOOKS
One crochet hook size US H/8 (5 mm)
Change hook size if necessary to obtain correct gauge.

GAUGE
20 sts and 20 rows = 4" (10 cm) in Seed stitch

STITCH PATTERN

SEED STITCH (odd number of sts + 1 ch; 2-row repeat)
Set-Up Row: Sc in second ch from hook, *ch 1, skip next ch, sc in next ch; repeat from * to end, turn.
Row 1: Ch 2 (counts as 1 sc and ch-1 sp), *sc in ch-1 sp, skip next sc, ch 1; repeat from *, sc in last ch, turn.
Row 2: Ch 1, sc in first ch-1 sp, *ch 1, skip next sc, sc in next ch-1 sp; repeat from * to end, turn.
Repeat Rows 1 and 2 for Seed st.

BACK

Using MC, ch 48 (52, 58, 62, 66, 76). Begin Seed st; work even until piece measures 3 (3, 3, 3½, 3½, 4)" from the beginning—47 (51, 57, 61, 65, 75) sts.

Shape Armholes (RS): Slip st into first 4 sts of row, work to last 4 sts, turn.
Decrease Row: Ch 1, pull a loop through first sc, next ch and next sc, yo and pull through 3 loops on hook (2 sts decreased), work to end. Repeat Decrease Row 3 times—31 (35, 41, 45, 49, 59) sts remain. Work even until armhole measures 4½ (4¾, 5, 5½, 6, 6½)", ending with a WS row. Fasten off.

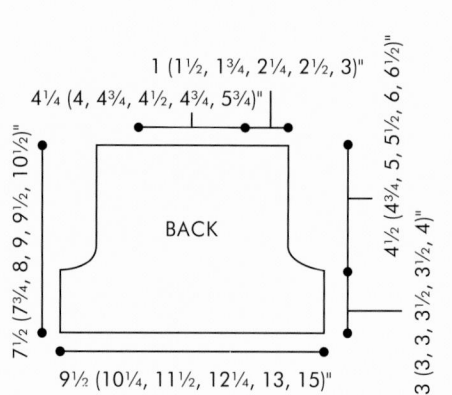

1 (1½, 1¾, 2¼, 2½, 3)"

4¼ (4, 4¾, 4½, 4¾, 5¾)"

7½ (7¾, 8, 9, 9½, 10½)"

BACK

4½ (4¾, 5, 5½, 6, 6½)"

3 (3, 3, 3½, 3½, 4)"

9½ (10¼, 11½, 12¼, 13, 15)"

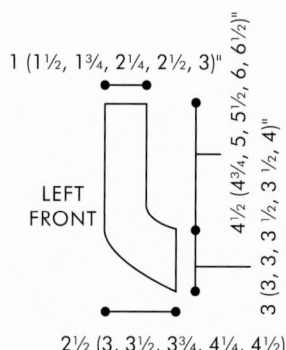

1 (1½, 1¾, 2¼, 2½, 3)"

LEFT FRONT

4½ (4¾, 5, 5½, 6, 6½)"

3 (3, 3 ½, 3 ½, 4)"

2½ (3, 3½, 3¾, 4¼, 4½)"

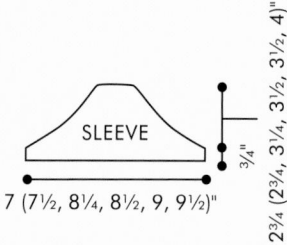

SLEEVE

¾"

2¾ (2¾, 3¼, 3½, 3½, 4)"

7 (7½, 8¼, 8½, 9, 9½)"

LEFT FRONT

Using MC, ch 6. Begin Seed st; work even for 1 row—5 sts.

SHAPING LEFT FRONT

Increase Row (WS): Continuing in Seed st, ch 2, [sc, ch 1, sc] in ch-1 sp (2 sts increased), work to end—7 sts. Repeat Increase Row every other row 3 (4, 5, 6, 7, 8) times—13 (15, 17, 19, 21, 23) sts. Work even until piece measures 3 (3, 3, 3½, 3½, 4)" from the beginning, ending with WS row. Shape armhole as for Back—5 (7, 9, 11, 13, 15) sts remain. Work even until armhole measures same as for Back, ending with a WS row. Fasten off.

RIGHT FRONT

Work as for Left Front, reversing all shaping.

SLEEVES

Using MC, ch 36 (38, 42, 44, 46, 48). Begin Seed st; work even for 4 rows—35 (37, 41, 43, 45, 47) sts.

SHAPE CAP

Next Row (RS): Slip st into first 2 sts of row, work to last 2 sts, turn—31 (33, 37, 39, 41, 43) sts remain. Work even for 3 rows.
Decrease Row (RS): Ch 1, pull a loop through first sc, next ch and next sc, yo and pull through 3 loops on hook (2 sts decreased), work to end. Repeat Decrease Row 7 (7, 9, 11, 11, 13) times.
Slip st into first 2 (3, 3, 2, 3, 2) sts of row, work to last 2 (3, 3, 2, 3, 2) sts, turn—11 sts remain. Work even for 1 row. Fasten off.

FINISHING

Sew shoulder and side seams.

Front Ruffle: With RS facing, using MC, join yarn with slip st at right shoulder, ch 3, work 165 (171, 180, 192, 204, 225) dc along Back neck, down Right Front edge, along bottom Back edge, then up Left Front edge, join with a slip st in top of first dc.
Next Rnd: Ch 3, *dc in first dc, 2 dc in next dc; repeat from * around, join with a slip st in top of ch-3.
Next Rnd: Change to A; ch 1, sc in next dc and in each dc around, join with a slip st to first dc. Fasten off.

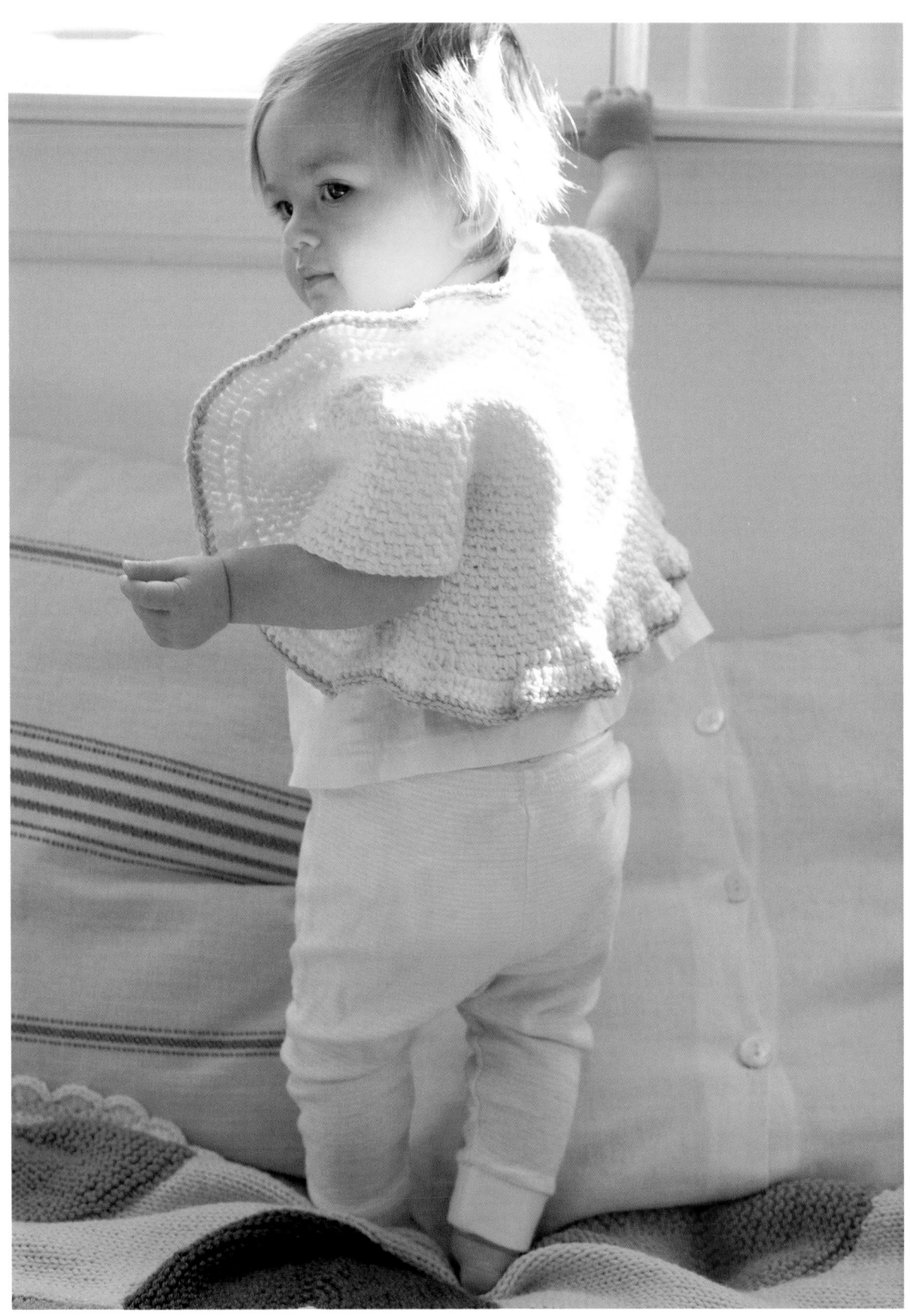

Jet Age
Cardigan

A stylized orange jet zooms across the back of this simple collared cardigan, and gray tipping adds the feeling of a varsity jacket. If you've never knit an intarsia design before, this is a great place to start—a few rows of effort yield bold, fun results.

SIZES
12 (18, 24) months

FINISHED MEASUREMENTS
22 (24¼, 27½)" chest

YARN
Berroco Vintage Chunky (50% acrylic / 40% wool / 10% nylon; 100 grams / 130 yards): 3 hanks #6100 Snow Day (A); 1 hank each #6164 Tang (B) and #6107 Cracked Pepper (C)

NEEDLES
One pair straight needles size US 10 (6 mm)
One pair straight needles size US 8 (5 mm)
Change needle size if necessary to obtain correct gauge.

NOTIONS
Stitch markers; five 1" buttons

GAUGE
14 sts and 21 rows = 4" (10 cm) in Stockinette stitch (St st), using larger needles

STITCH PATTERN
1X1 RIB (odd number of sts; 1-row repeat)
Row 1 (RS): K1, *p1, k1; repeat from * to end.
Row 2: Knit the knit sts and purl the purl sts as they face you. Repeat Row 2 for 1x1 Rib.

NOTE
Chart is worked using the Intarsia Colorwork Method (see Special Techniques, page 156).

BACK
Using smaller needles and A, CO 39 (43, 49) sts. Begin 1x1 Rib; work for 2", ending with a WS row and decreasing 1 st on last row—38 (42, 48) sts remain. Change to larger needles and St st; work even until piece measures 6½ (6½, 7)" from the beginning, ending with a WS row.
Next Row (RS): K5 (7, 10), place marker (pm), work Chart over 28 sts, pm, knit to end. Work even until piece measures 7½ (7½, 8)" from the beginning, ending with a WS row.

SHAPE ARMHOLES
Next Row (RS): Continuing to work Chart, BO 2 sts at beginning of next 2 rows, then decrease 1 st each side every other row 2 (4, 6) times, as follows: K1, k2tog, work to last 3 sts, ssk, k1—30 (30, 32) sts remain. AT THE SAME TIME, when Chart is complete, change to A and work even until armholes measure 4½ (4¾, 5)", ending with a WS row.

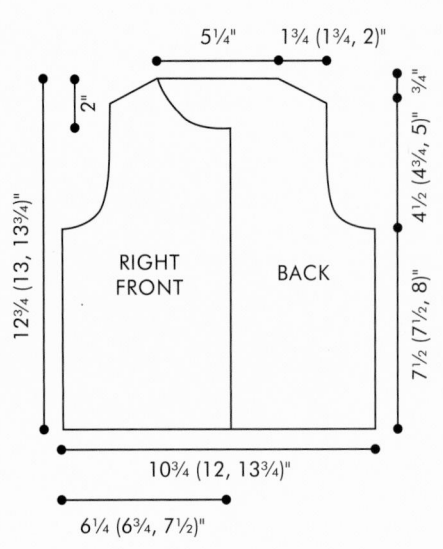

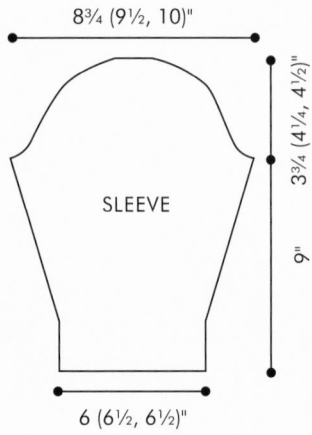

SHAPE SHOULDERS

Next Row (RS): BO 3 (3, 4) sts at beginning of next 2 rows, then 3 sts at beginning of next 2 rows. BO remaining 18 sts for Back neck.

RIGHT FRONT

With smaller needles and A, CO 23 (25, 27) sts.

Next Row (RS): K4 [edge sts, keep in Garter st (knit every row)], pm, work in 1x1 Rib to end. Working sts at Front edge in Garter st, work even for 2", ending with a WS row and decreasing 1 st on last row—22 (24, 26) sts remain.

Next Row (RS): Change to larger needles. Work 4 sts in Garter st, work in St st to end. Work even until piece measures 7½ (7½, 8)" from the beginning, ending with a RS row.

SHAPE ARMHOLE

Next Row(WS): BO 2 sts at armhole edge once, then decrease 1 st every other row 2 (4, 6) times, as follows: Work to last 3 sts, ssk, k1—18 sts remain. Work even until armhole measures 3¼ (3½, 3¾)", ending with a WS row.

SHAPE NECK

Next Row (RS): BO 6 (6, 5) sts at neck edge once, then decrease 1 st at neck edge every row 6 times, as follows: On RS rows, k1, k2tog, work to end; on WS rows, work to last 3 sts, p2tog, p1—6 (6, 7) sts remain. Work even until armhole measures 4½ (4¾, 5)", ending with a RS row.

Shape Shoulder (WS): BO 3 (3, 4) sts at armhole edge once, then 3 sts once. Place markers for 5 buttons on Front Garter st band, the first 1" above bottom edge, the last ½" below neck shaping, and the remaining 3 evenly spaced between.

LEFT FRONT

With smaller needles and A, CO 23 (25, 27) sts.

Next Row (RS): Work 1x1 Rib to last 4 sts, pm, k4 (edge sts, keep in Garter st). Working sts at Front edge in Garter st, work even for 1", ending with a WS row.

Buttonhole Row (RS): Work to last 4 sts, k2tog, yo, k2. Work even until piece measures 2" from the beginning, ending with a WS row and decreasing 1 st on last row—22 (24, 26) sts remain.

Next Row (RS): Change to larger needles. Complete as for Right Front, reversing all shaping and working 4 more buttonholes opposite markers on Right Front band.

CHART

KEY □ ▨ ▨
     A   B   C

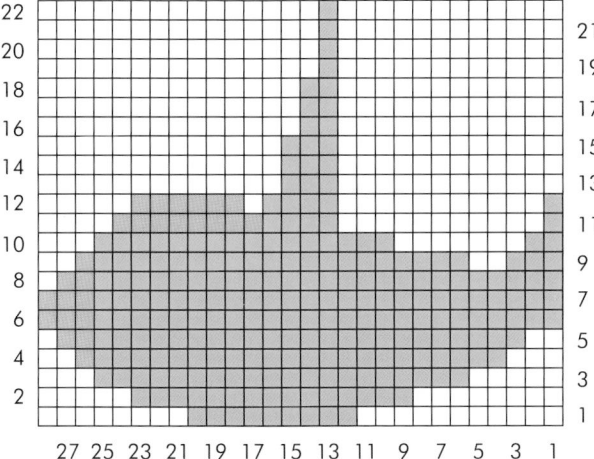

22
20
18
16
14
12
10
8
6
4
2

21
19
17
15
13
11
9
7
5
3
1

27 25 23 21 19 17 15 13 11 9 7 5 3 1

SLEEVE

With smaller needles and C, CO 21 (23, 23) sts. Begin 1x1 Rib; work even for 2 rows. Change to A; work even until piece measures 2" from the beginning, ending with a WS row. Change to larger needles and St st; work even until piece measures 3" from the beginning, ending with a WS row.

SHAPE SLEEVE

Increase Row (RS): Increase 1 st each side this row, then every 6 rows 4 (4, 5) times, as follows: K1, M1, knit to last st, M1, k1—31 (33, 35) sts. Work even until piece measures 9" from the beginning, ending with a WS row.

SHAPE CAP

Next Row (RS): BO 2 sts at beginning of next 2 rows, decrease 1 st each side every other row 8 (9, 10) times, as follows: K1, k2tog, work to last 3 sts, ssk, k1. Purl 1 row. BO 3 sts at beginning of next 2 rows. BO remaining 5 sts.

Sew shoulder seams. Set in Sleeves. Sew side and Sleeve seams.

Collar: With RS facing, using smaller needles and A, beginning 2 sts in from Right Front edge, pick up and knit 47 sts evenly around neck edge, ending 2 sts in from Left Front edge. Begin 1x1 Rib; work even until piece measures 1½" from pick-up row, ending with a WS row. Change to larger needles; work even until piece measures 2¾" from pick-up row. Change to C; work even for 2 rows. BO all sts in 1x1 Rib. Sew buttons to Right Front at markers.

Moderne
Blanket

This blanket, inspired by the colors and geometric constructions of mid-twentieth-century artwork, is made up of twenty Garter-stitch blocks. Some blocks are worked in a solid color, while others are worked in multiple colors. Easy to tackle one square at a time, this afghan is fascinating to piece together.

FINISHED MEASUREMENTS
37" wide x 46¼" long
Blanket Square: 9¼" wide x 9¼" long

YARN
Berroco Comfort (50% super fine nylon / 50% super fine acrylic; 100 grams / 210 yards): 5 skeins #9702 Pearl (A); 1 skein each #9724 Pumpkin (B), #9733 Turquoise (C), #9764 Lidfors (D), #9717 Raspberry Coulis (E), and #9753 Aegean Sea (F)

NEEDLES
One pair straight needles size US 9 (5.5 mm)
Change needle size if necessary to obtain correct gauge.

GAUGE
18 sts and 36 rows = 4" (10 cm) in Garter stitch (knit every row)

SQUARES 1, 10, 16, AND 19
Using A, CO 42 sts. Knit 83 rows. BO all sts knitwise.

SQUARES 2 AND 20
Using A, CO 42 sts. Knit 42 rows.
Next Row: Using A, k21, using C, k21. Continuing in colors as established, knit 40 rows. BO all sts knitwise.

SQUARE 3
Using C, CO 14 sts, using E, CO 14 sts, using A, CO 14 sts—42 sts. Continuing in colors as established, knit 28 rows.
Next Row: Using A, k28, using D, k14. Continuing in colors as established, knit 27 rows.
Next Row: Using A, k14, using F, k14, using A, k14. Continuing in colors as established, knit 26 rows. BO all sts knitwise.

SQUARES 4 AND 6
Using A, CO 42 sts. Knit 42 rows.
Next Row: Using A, k21, using B, k21. Continuing in colors as established, knit 40 rows. BO all sts knitwise.

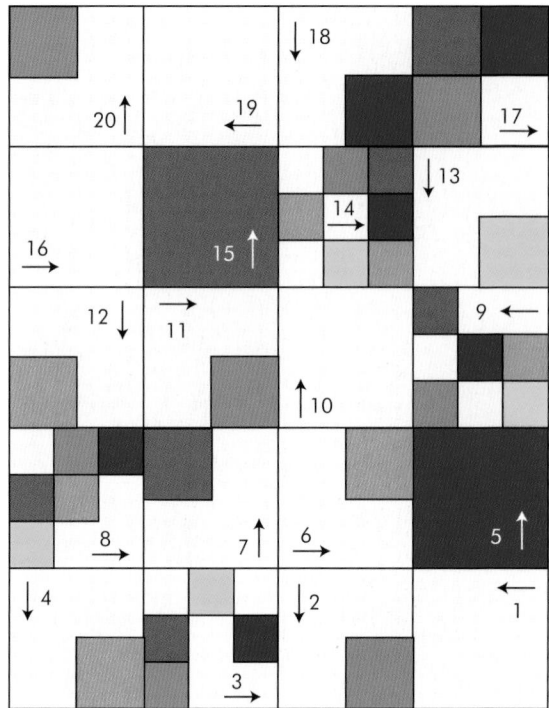

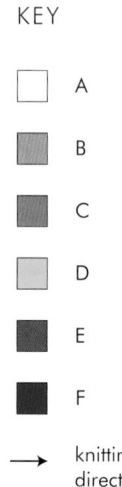

KEY

☐ A

▨ B

▨ C

▨ D

▨ E

▨ F

→ knitting direction

SQUARE 5
Using F, work as for Square 1.

SQUARE 7
Using A, CO 42 sts. Knit 42 rows.
Next Row: Using A, k21, using E, k21. Continuing in colors as established, knit 40 rows. BO all sts knitwise.

SQUARE 8
Using D, CO 14 sts, using E, CO 14 sts, using A, CO 14 sts—42 sts. Continuing in colors as established, knit 28 rows.
Next Row: Using A, k14, using B, k14, using C, k14. Continuing in colors as established, knit 27 rows.
Next Row: Using A, k28, using F, k14. Continuing in colors as established, knit 26 rows. BO all sts knitwise.

SQUARE 9
Using A, CO 14 sts, using B, CO 14 sts, using D, CO 14 sts—42 sts. Continuing in colors as established, knit 28 rows.

Next Row: Using A, k14, using F, k14, using A, k14. Continuing in colors as established, knit 27 rows.
Next Row: Using E, k14, using A, k14, using C, k14. Continuing in colors as established, knit 26 rows. BO all sts knitwise.

SQUARE 11
Using A, CO 42 sts. Knit 42 rows.
Next Row: Using C, k21, using A, k21. Continuing in colors as established, knit 40 rows. BO all sts knitwise.

SQUARE 12
Using A, CO 42 sts. Knit 42 rows.
Next Row: Using B, k21, using A, k21. Continuing in colors as established, knit 40 rows. BO all sts knitwise.

SQUARE 13
Using A, CO 42 sts. Knit 42 rows.
Next Row: Using A, k21, using D, k21. Continuing in colors as established, knit 40 rows. BO all sts knitwise.

SQUARE 14

Using A, CO 14 sts,
using B, CO 14 sts, using
A, CO 14 sts—42 sts.
Continuing in colors as
established, knit 28 rows.
Next Row: Using D, k14,
using A, k14, using C, k14.
Continuing in colors as
established, knit 27 rows.
Next Row: Using B, k14,
using F, k14, using E, k14.
Continuing in colors as
established, knit 26 rows.
BO all sts knitwise.

SQUARE 15

Using E, work as for
Square 1.

SQUARE 17

Using C, CO 21 sts, using
E, CO 21 sts—42 sts.
Knit 42 rows.
Next Row: Using A, k21,
using F, k21. Continuing in
colors as established, knit
40 rows. BO all sts knitwise.

SQUARE 18

Using A, CO 42 sts. Knit
42 rows.
Next Row: Using A, k21,
using F, k21. Continuing in
colors as established, knit
40 rows. BO all sts knitwise.

FINISHING

Sew Squares together,
following Assembly
Diagram.

Block lightly (see Special
Techniques, page 156).

Solaria Blanket

To make this cheerful circular blanket, one cable pattern is repeated sixteen times, resulting in an amazing profusion of texture. Diamonds and cables intertwine, forming negative spaces that are as interesting as the raised design.

FINISHED MEASUREMENTS
36" diameter

YARN
Berroco Comfort Chunky (50% super fine nylon / 50% super fine acrylic; 100 grams / 150 yards): 6 skeins #5743 Goldenrod

NEEDLES
One 36" (90 cm) long circular (circ) needle size US 10½ (6.5 mm)
One 24" (60 cm) long circular needle size US 10½ (6.5 mm)
One set of five double-pointed needles (dpn) size US 10½ (6.5 mm)
Change needle size if necessary to obtain correct gauge.

NOTIONS
Stitch markers; cable needle (cn)

GAUGE
13 sts and 20 rows = 4" (10 cm) in Stockinette stitch (St st)

BLANKET
Using longer circ needle, CO 416 sts. Do not join. Knit 2 rows. Join for working in the rnd, being careful not to twist sts; pm for beginning of rnd.

Next Rnd: *Work Cable Pattern from Chart over 26 sts, pm; repeat from * to end, omitting pm on final repeat. Work even until entire Chart has been completed, working decreases as indicated in Chart—16 sts remain. *Note: Change to shorter circ needle, then dpns, when necessary for number of sts on needle.*

Next Rnd: *K2tog; repeat from * to end—8 sts remain. Cut yarn, leaving an 8" tail; thread tail through remaining sts, pull tight, and fasten off.

FINISHING
Using CO tail, sew edges of first 2 rows together.

Block lightly (see Special Techniques, page 156).

CABLE PATTERN

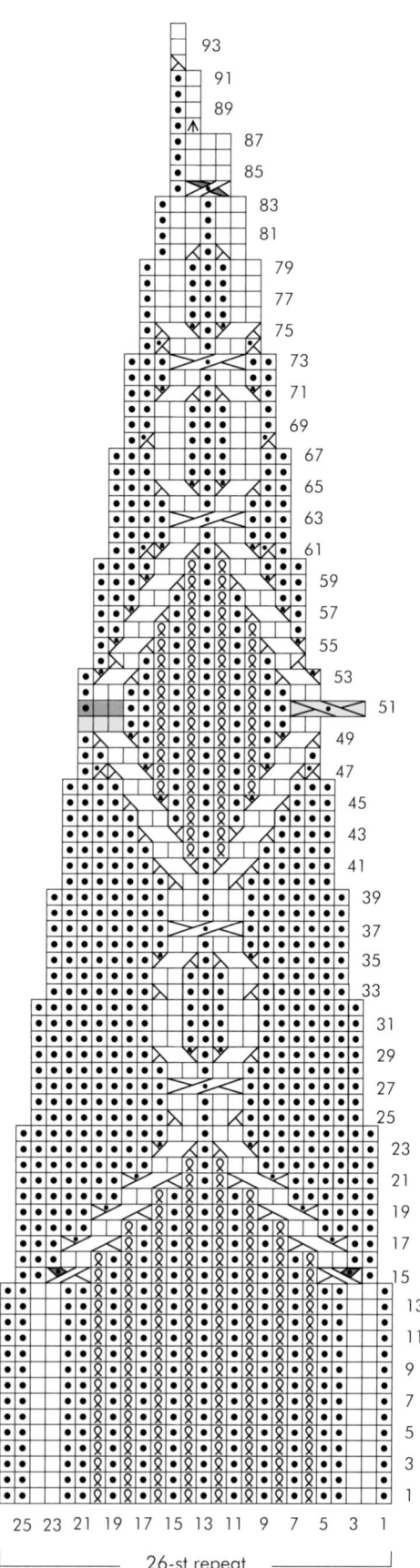

93
91
89
87
85
83
81
79
77
75
73
71
69
67
65
63
61
59
57
55
53
51
49
47
45
43
41
39
37
35
33
31
29
27
25
23
21
19
17
15
13
11
9
7
5
3
1

25 23 21 19 17 15 13 11 9 7 5 3 1

|⎿———— 26-st repeat ————⏌|

KEY

☐	Knit
⊡	Purl
⊠	K1-tbl
⧅	K2tog
⧄	Ssk
⊠	P2tog
⬆	K3tog

⟋⟍ Slip 2 sts to cn and hold to front, k1, k2 from cn.

⟋⟍ Slip 1 st to cn and hold to back, k2, k1 from cn.

⟋⟍ Slip 2 sts to cn and hold to front, p1, k2 from cn.

⟋⟍ Slip 1 st to cn and hold to back, k2, p1 from cn.

⟋⟍ Slip 2 sts to cn and hold to front, p2tog, k2 from cn.

⟋⟍ Slip 2 sts to cn and hold to back, k2, p2tog from cn.

⟋⟍ Slip 3 sts to cn and hold to back, k2tog, (p1, k2tog) from cn.

▭▭▭ On final repeat of Rnd 50, end rnd before these 3 sts. Work them at the beginning of Rnd 51 as indicated on Rnd 51.

⬛▭ Work on final repeat of Rnd 51 only.

⟋▭⟍ Slip 2 sts to cn and hold to front, p2, k2 from cn.

⟋▭⟍ Slip 2 sts to cn and hold to back, k2, p2 from cn.

⟋▭▭⟍ Slip 3 sts to cn and hold to back, k2, (p1, k2) from cn.

⟋▭⟍ Slip 3 sts to cn and hold to front, k2, p1, k2 from cn.

⟋▭⟍ On first repeat, work over last 3 sts of Rnd 50 and first 2 sts of Rnd 51. Slip 3 sts to cn and hold to front, remove marker, k2, [p1, replace marker, k2 from cn].

Sideways Cardigan

Much like patterned sock yarn, the yarn used for this easy cardigan works up in stripes and dots, doing all the color changes for you. While working from cuff to cuff in the simplest of crochet stitches, it's fun to see the patterns emerge and wonder what color will be next.

SIZES
3 (6, 9, 12, 18, 24) months

FINISHED MEASUREMENTS
19 (21, 22, 23, 24, 26)"

YARN
Berroco Comfort DK (50% super fine nylon / 50% super fine acrylic; 50 grams / 178 yards): 3 (3, 3, 4, 4, 4) skeins #2856 Balance Beam

CROCHET HOOKS
One crochet hook size US F/5 (3.75 mm)
Change hook size if necessary to obtain correct gauge.

NOTIONS
Five ⅝" buttons

GAUGE
22 sts and 26 rows = 4" (10 cm) in Ridged Single Crochet (Ridged sc)

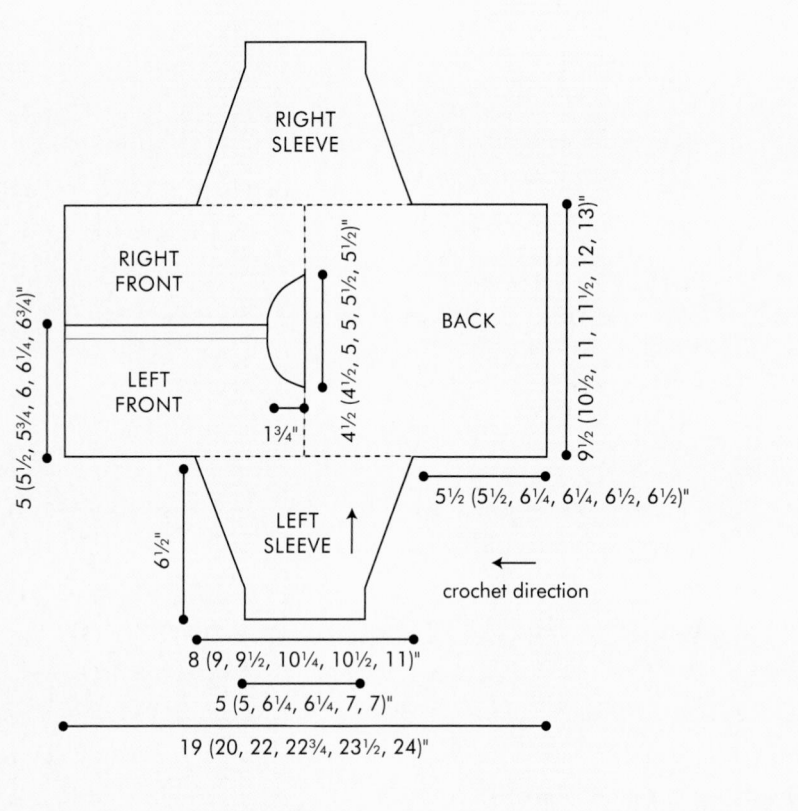

RIGHT SLEEVE

RIGHT FRONT

LEFT FRONT

BACK

$4\frac{1}{2}$ ($4\frac{1}{2}$, 5, $5\frac{1}{2}$, $5\frac{1}{2}$)"

$1\frac{3}{4}$"

5 ($5\frac{1}{2}$, $5\frac{3}{4}$, 6, $6\frac{1}{4}$, $6\frac{3}{4}$)"

$9\frac{1}{2}$ ($10\frac{1}{2}$, 11, $11\frac{1}{2}$, 12, 13)"

$5\frac{1}{2}$ ($5\frac{1}{2}$, $6\frac{1}{4}$, $6\frac{1}{4}$, $6\frac{1}{2}$, $6\frac{1}{2}$)"

LEFT SLEEVE

$6\frac{1}{2}$"

← crochet direction

8 (9, $9\frac{1}{2}$, $10\frac{1}{4}$, $10\frac{1}{2}$, 11)"

5 (5, $6\frac{1}{4}$, $6\frac{1}{4}$, 7, 7)"

19 (20, 22, $22\frac{3}{4}$, $23\frac{1}{2}$, 24)"

STITCH PATTERN

RIDGED SINGLE CROCHET (any number of sts + 1 ch; 2-row repeat)

Set-Up Row (WS): Sc in second ch from hook and in each ch to end, turn.

Row 1: Ch 1, *sc-tbl in each sc to end, turn.

Row 2: Ch 1, *sc-tfl in each sc to end, turn.

Repeat Rows 1 and 2 for Ridged sc.

NOTE

Piece is worked sideways from Left Sleeve to Right Sleeve.

LEFT SLEEVE

Ch 29 (29, 35, 35, 39, 39). Begin Ridged sc; work even for 8 rows—28 (28, 34, 34, 38, 38) sc.

SHAPE SLEEVE

Increase Row (RS): Increase 1 st each side this row, then every other row 7 (10, 8, 10, 9, 10) times, as follows: Work 2 sc in the same st, work to last st, work 2 sc in the same st—44 (50, 52, 56, 58, 60) sc. Work even until piece measures $6\frac{1}{2}$" from the beginning, ending with a WS row. Take note of number of rows worked after last Increase Row.

BODY

Next Row (RS): Ch 31 (31, 35, 35, 37, 37), turn, work sc in second ch from hook and in ch, then work in pattern as established to end, ch 31 (31, 35, 35, 37, 37), turn, work sc in second ch from hook and in each ch, then work in pattern as established to end—104 (110, 120, 124, 130, 132) sc. Work even until piece measures $2\frac{1}{2}$ (3, 3, $3\frac{1}{4}$, $3\frac{1}{4}$, $3\frac{3}{4}$)" from beginning of Body, ending with a WS row.

SHAPE BACK NECK

Next Row (RS): Work 52 (55, 60, 62, 65, 66) sts, turn. Working on Back sts only, work even until Back neck measures 4½ (4½, 5, 5, 5½, 5½)", ending with a RS row. Cut yarn.

LEFT FRONT
SHAPE NECK

Next Row (RS): With RS facing, rejoin yarn to Front neck edge, slip st into first 4 sts of Left Front, work to end. Slip 3 sts at Front neck edge every RS row once, 2 sts once, then 1 st once—42 (45, 50, 52, 55, 56) sc remain. Work even until piece measures 4¾ (5¼, 5½, 5¾, 6, 6½)" from beginning of Body, ending with a WS row. Place markers for 5 buttonholes, the first 2 sts from neck edge, the last 2 sts from the bottom edge, and 3 more evenly spaced between.
Buttonhole Row (RS): Work even, working ch 2 and sk 2 at each marker. Work even for 1 row, working 2 sc in each ch-2 sp. Fasten off.

RIGHT FRONT

Ch 43 (46, 51, 53, 56, 57). Begin Ridged sc; work even until piece measures 1½ (1½, 1¾, 1¾, 2, 2)", ending with a WS row—42 (45, 50, 52, 55, 56) sc.

SHAPE NECK

Increase Row 1 (RS): Ch 2, turn, work sc in second ch from hook, work to end.
Increase Row 2 (WS): Work to end, ch 3, turn, work sc in second and third ch from hook, work to end.
Increase Row 3 (WS): Work to end, ch 4, turn, work sc in second, third, and fourth ch from hook, work to end.
Increase Row 4 (WS): Work to end, ch 5, turn, work sc in second, third, fourth, and fifth ch from hook, work to end—52 (55, 60, 62, 65, 66).
Join Front and Back (WS): Work to end of Front, work across Back sts to end—104 (110, 120, 124, 130, 132) sts. Work even until piece measures 9½ (10½, 11, 11½, 12, 13)" from beginning of Body, ending with a WS row.

RIGHT SLEEVE

Next Row (RS): Slip st into first 30 (30, 34, 34, 36, 36) sts, work next 44 (50, 52, 56, 58, 60) sts, turn—44 (50, 52, 56, 58, 60) sts remain. Work even for number of rows worked on Left Sleeve after last Increase Row.

SHAPE SLEEVE

Decrease Row: Decrease 2 st at beginning and end of this row, then every other row 7 (10, 8, 10, 9, 10) times, as follows: Sc2tog, work to last 2 sts, sc2tog—28 (28, 34, 34, 38, 38) sc remain. Work even until piece measures same as for Left Sleeve. Fasten off.

FINISHING

Collar: With WS of Left Front facing, beginning ¼" in from Left Front edge, work 62 (68, 75, 79, 86, 94) sc evenly along Left Front neck, Back neck, then Right Front neck, ending ¼" before Right Front neck edge. Begin Ridged sc; work even for 3". Fasten off.

Sew side and Sleeve seams. Sew buttons to Right Front opposite buttonholes.

Rag Rug Blanket

The inspiration for this knitted blanket was a Turkish rag rug. Sewn down the center, this blanket has a charming contrast between a lighter, faded half and a more saturated side. We were able to simulate the subtle variations in color by working alternating rows in variegated and solid shades of Comfort yarn.

FINISHED MEASUREMENTS
36" wide x 42" long

YARN
Berroco Comfort (50% super fine nylon / 50% super fine acrylic; 100 grams / 210 yards): 1 skein each #9728 Raspberry Sorbet (A), #9785 Falseberry Heather (B), #9838 Raspberry Tart (C), #9807 Military Mix (D), #9805 Berry Mix (E), #9833 Security Blanket (F), #9753 Aegean Sea (G), #9715 Lavender Frost (H), #9794 Wild Raspberry Heather (I), #9744 Teal (J), and #9748 Aunt Martha Green (K).

NEEDLES
One pair straight needles size US 9 (5.5 mm)
Change needle size if necessary to obtain correct gauge.

GAUGE
18 sts and 24 rows = 4" (10 cm) in Stockinette st (St st)

STITCH PATTERNS
STRIP 1 COLOR SEQUENCE
*Work 8 rows C, 8 rows D, 8 rows E, 8 rows F, 12 rows G, 8 rows H, 8 rows I, 8 rows A, then 8 rows B; repeat from * for Strip 1 Color Sequence.

STRIP 2 COLOR SEQUENCE
*Work 10 rows J, 10 rows D, 4 rows G, 10 rows H, 10 rows K, 10 rows F, 10 rows A, then 10 rows B; repeat from * for Strip 2 Color Sequence.

BLANKET
STRIP 1
Using A, CO 82 sts. Begin Garter st (knit every row); work even for 8 rows. Change to B.
Row 1 (RS): Knit.
Row 2: Purl to last 6 sts, k6 (edge sts, keep in Garter st).
Repeat Rows 1 and 2 three times. Change to Strip 1 Color Sequence. Working 6 sts at right-hand edge of Strip in Garter st as established, and remaining sts in St st, work even until

piece measures 40¾" from the beginning, ending with a WS row. Continuing with Color Sequence, change to Garter st; work even for 8 rows. BO all sts.

STRIP 2
Using B, CO 82 sts. Begin Garter st; work even for 8 rows.
Row 1 (RS): Knit.
Row 2: K6 (edge sts, keep in Garter st), purl to end.
Change to Strip 2 Color Sequence. Working 6 sts at left-hand edge of Strip in Garter st as established, and remaining sts in

St st, work even until piece measures 40¾" from the beginning, ending with a WS row. Continuing with Color Sequence, change to Garter st; work even for 8 rows. BO all sts.

FINISHING
Sew Strips together, sewing through half of the edge st on each Strip to minimize the seam.

Block lightly (see Special Techniques, page 156).

Deanna
Jumper

A jumper is one of the most versatile items you can make for a little girl. Layered over tights and a turtleneck in the winter or a little t-shirt in the summer, the jumper is an easy wardrobe option. Children tend to grow in height faster than they grow around, so this dress will start out longish on a baby and will become a shorter dress as she grows (we left the armholes plenty deep to allow for this). A band of contrasting trim highlights the yoke, and huge buttons give the jumper a ragamuffin flair.

SIZES
3 (6, 9, 12, 18, 24) months

FINISHED MEASUREMENTS
22 (24, 26, 28, 30, 34)" chest

YARN
Berroco Vintage (50% acrylic / 40% wool / 10% nylon; 100 grams / 217 yards): 2 (2, 2, 3, 3, 3) hanks #5187 Dungaree (MC); 1 hank #5104 Mushroom (A)

CROCHET HOOKS
One crochet hook size US I/9 (5.5 mm)
One crochet hook size US H/8 (5 mm)
Change hook size if necessary to obtain correct gauge.

NOTIONS
Two 1½" buttons

GAUGE
20 sts and 16 rows = 4" (10 cm) in Open Single Crochet (Open sc), using larger hook

STITCH PATTERN
OPEN SINGLE CROCHET (odd number of sts + 1 ch; 1-row repeat)
Set-Up Row: Sc in second ch from hook, *ch 1, skip next ch, sc in next ch; repeat from * to end, turn.
All Rows: Ch 1, sc in first sc, *ch 1, skip ch-1 sp, sc in next sc; repeat from * to end, turn.

BACK
Using larger crochet hook and MC, ch 56 (62, 66, 72, 76, 86). Begin Open sc; work even until piece measures 8 (9, 9, 10, 10, 11)" from the beginning, ending with a WS row—55 (61, 65, 71, 75, 85) sts remain.

SHAPE ARMHOLES
Next Row (RS): Slip st in first 3 (4, 4, 4, 4, 3) sts, work in Open sc to last 3 (4, 4, 4, 4, 3) sts, turn—49 (53, 57, 63, 67, 79) sts remain. Work even for 1 row.
Next Row (RS): Decrease 1 st each side this row, then every row 3 times—41 (45, 49, 55, 59, 71) sts remain. Work even until piece measures 10 (11, 11, 12, 12, 13)" from the beginning, ending with a WS row.

BODICE

Change to A and smaller crochet hook.

Row 1 (RS): Ch 1, sc in first 2 sc, *pull up a loop in each of next 2 sts, yo and pull through all loops on hook; repeat from * to last st, sc in last st, turn—22 (24, 26, 29, 31, 37) sts remain.

Row 2: Ch 1, working through back loop, sc in each sc across.

Row 3: Change to MC. Repeat Row 2.

Row 4: Ch 1, working through both loops, sc in each sc across. Work even in sc until piece measures 12 (13, 13, 14, 14, 15)" from the beginning, ending with a WS row.

STRAPS

Right Strap (RS): Ch 1, sc in first 6 sc, turn leaving remaining sts unworked. Work even in sc until Strap measures 5", ending with a WS row.

Buttonhole Row (RS): Ch 1, sc in first 2 sts, ch 2, skip 2 sc, sc in last 2 sc, turn.

Next Row: Ch 1, sc evenly across, working 2 sc in ch-2 sp, turn. Work even in sc until strap measures 6". Fasten off.

Left Strap: Rejoin MC to last 6 sts of Bodice. Work in sc and complete as for Right Strap.

FRONT

Work as for Back to end of Bodice. Fasten off.

FINISHING

Sew side seams. Sew buttons to Front Bodice.

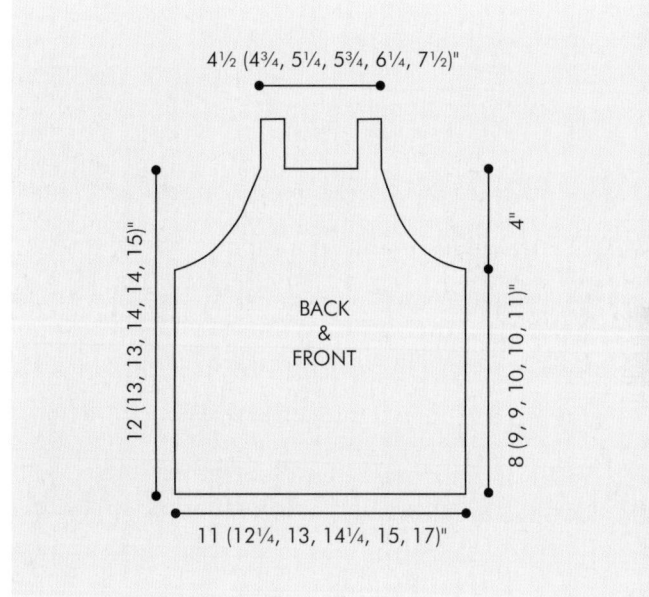

4½ (4¾, 5¼, 5¾, 6¼, 7½)"

12 (13, 13, 14, 14, 15)"

4"

8 (9, 9, 10, 10, 11)"

BACK & FRONT

11 (12¼, 13, 14¼, 15, 17)"

Judi Blanket

Among the many talents my grandmother picked up from her mother was the ability to take a worn-out textile and transform it into something beautiful with a few simple embroidery stitches. This blanket is an homage to this time-honored skill. Simple ecru and white borders appear as though they are pieced from two separate items, and a bit of contrasting embroidery—running stitches and cross stitches—embellish the corners, elevating a blanket that might otherwise be considered plain.

FINISHED MEASUREMENTS
38" wide x 44" long

YARN
Berroco Vintage (50% acrylic / 40% wool / 10% nylon; 100 grams / 217 yards): 5 hanks #5104 Mushroom (A); 2 hanks #5101 Mochi (B); 1 hank each #5194 Breezeway (C) and #5187 Dungaree (D)

CROCHET HOOKS
One Tunisian (Afghan) crochet hook size US I/9 (5.5 mm)
One crochet hook size US I/9 (5.5 mm)
Change hook size if necessary to obtain correct gauge.

NOTIONS
Tapestry needle

GAUGE
16 sts and 16 rows = 4" (10 cm) in Tunisian Simple Stitch (Tss), using Tunisian crochet hook

CHART A

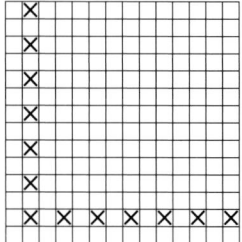

CHART B

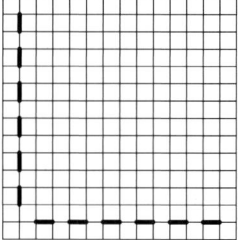

KEY

☐ Background st

✕ Cross st

— Running st

STITCH PATTERN

TUNISIAN SIMPLE STITCH (TSS) (any number of sts, 1-row repeat)

Note: All rows are RS rows. Each row is comprised of a Forward Pass (Fwd) and a Return Pass (Rtn).

With crochet hook, work a foundation ch.

Row 1: Fwd: Insert hook in second ch from hook, yo and pull up a loop, then yo and pull up a loop in each ch across, leaving all loops on hook. Rtn: Yo and pull through first loop on hook, *yo and pull through 2 loops on hook; repeat from * across—1 loop left on hook counts as first st of next row.

Row 2: Fwd: *Insert hook under first vertical thread on row just worked from right to left, yo, pull up a loop; repeat from * across, leaving all loops on hook. Rtn: Yo and pull through first loop on hook, *yo and pull through 2 loops on hook; repeat from * across—1 loop left on hook counts as first st of next row. Repeat Row 2 for Tunisian Simple Stitch.

CENTER SECTION

Using Tunisian crochet hook and A, ch 81. Begin Tss; work even until piece measures 26" from the beginning. Fasten off.

FIRST SIDE BORDERS

With RS facing and B, pick up 104 loops evenly spaced across one long side of Center Section. Begin Tss; work even for 4" Fasten off. Repeat for opposite side.

FIRST END BORDERS

With RS facing and B, pick up 112 loops evenly spaced across lower edge of Center Section, including Side Borders. Begin Tss; work even for 4". Fasten off. Repeat for opposite end.

SECOND SIDE BORDERS

With RS facing and A, pick up 136 loops evenly spaced across Side Border, including End Borders. Begin Tss; work even for 4".

Last Row: *Insert hook under first vertical thread on row as if to work a Tss, yo and pull up through st and loop on hook (slip st made); repeat from * across. Fasten off. Repeat for opposite side.

SECOND END BORDERS

With RS facing and A, pick up 144 loops evenly spaced across End Border, including Second Side Borders. Begin Tss; work even for 4".

Last Row: Work as for Last Row of Second Side Borders. Fasten off. Repeat for opposite end.

ASSEMBLY DIAGRAM

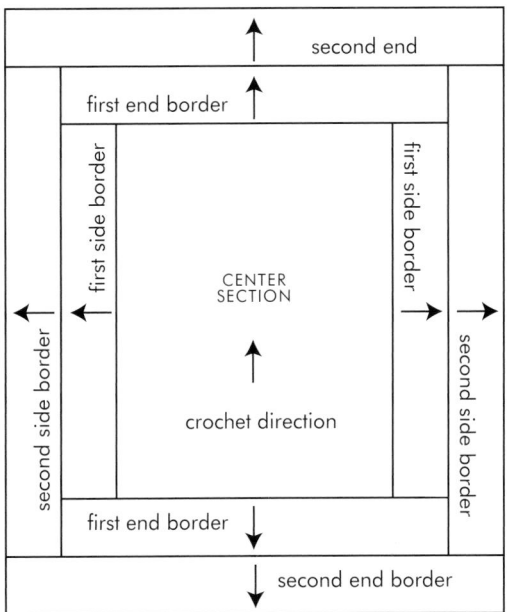

FINISHING

Using tapestry needle and C, work cross st embroidery for approximately 5" along all 4 corners of Center Section following Chart A. Using tapestry needle and D, work a running st along all outer edges of First Side and End Borders following Chart B. Using tapestry needle and C, work cross st embroidery along all outer edges of Second Side and End Borders following Chart A.

EDGING

Rnd 1: Using standard crochet hook, join A in any corner of Blanket, ch 1, *3 sc in corner st, sc across to next corner, skipping every eighth st on Blanket so Edging lies flat; repeat from * to end. Join with a slip st in first sc.

Rnds 2 and 3: Ch 1, sc in each sc around, working 3 sc in each corner sc, join with a slip st in first sc.

Rnd 4: Ch 1, working from left to right, reverse sc in each sc around, join with a slip st in first reverse sc. Fasten off.

Block lightly (see Special Techniques, page 156).

Rivulet Blanket

This classic knitted blanket is one to pass down through the generations. It is constructed with beautiful diamonds of cables and rib, and the rippling pattern seems sculpted, as though it has been carved from the fabric by a skilled artisan. Each new block is picked up along the side of the previous piece, greatly reducing the number of seams.

FINISHED MEASUREMENTS

40" wide x 48" long
Blanket Square: 8" wide x 8" long

YARN

Berroco Vintage DK (50% acrylic / 40% wool / 10% nylon; 100 grams / 288 yards): 8 hanks #2176 Pumpkin

NEEDLES

One pair straight needles size US 6 (4 mm)
Change needle size if necessary to obtain correct gauge.

NOTIONS

Cable needle (cn)

GAUGE

30½ sts and 32½ rows = 4" (10 cm) in Cable Pattern from Chart

STITCH PATTERN

2X2 RIB (multiple of 4 sts; 2-row repeat)
Row 1 (RS): K1, *p2, k2; repeat from * to last 3 sts, p2, k1.
Row 2: P1, *k2, p2; repeat from * to last 3 sts, k2, p1.
Repeat Rows 1 and 2 for 2x2 Rib.

BLANKET

STRIP 1

SQUARE 1
CO 64 sts. Begin 2x2 Rib; work even for 3 rows.
Decrease Row (WS): Work 11 sts, [p2tog, work 18 sts] twice, p2tog-tbl, work to end—61 sts remain.
Next Row: Change to Cable Pattern from Chart; work even until entire Cable Pattern is complete.
Increase Row (WS): Work 12 sts, M1-p, work 19 sts, M1-p, work 18 sts, M1-p, work to end—64 sts. Change to 2x2 Rib; work even for 3 rows. BO all sts in pattern.

SQUARE 2
With RS of Square 1 facing, pick up and knit 64 sts evenly along right-hand edge of Square 1. Begin 2x2 Rib, beginning with Row 2. Complete as for Square 1.

SQUARE 3
With RS of Square 2 facing, pick up and knit 64 sts evenly along left-hand edge of Square 2. Begin 2x2 Rib, beginning with Row 2. Complete as for Square 1.

STRIP 3	SQUARE 1	SQUARE 4	SQUARE 5	SQUARE 8	SQUARE 9
	SQUARE 2	SQUARE 3	SQUARE 6	SQUARE 7	SQUARE 10

seam →

STRIP 2	SQUARE 1	SQUARE 4	SQUARE 5	SQUARE 8	SQUARE 9
	SQUARE 2	SQUARE 3	SQUARE 6	SQUARE 7	SQUARE 10

seam →

STRIP 1

SQUARE 1 →	seam SQUARE 4 ↑ pick up	pick up SQUARE 5 →	seam SQUARE 8 ↑ pick up	pick up SQUARE 9 →
pick up SQUARE 2 ↓	pick up SQUARE 3 →	seam SQUARE 6 ↓	pick up SQUARE 7 →	seam SQUARE 10 ↓

pick up (above Square 2), pick up (above Square 6), pick up (above Square 10)

→
knitting direction

SQUARE 4
With RS of Square 3 facing, pick up and knit 64 sts evenly along left-hand edge of Square 3. Begin 2x2 Rib, beginning with Row 2. Complete as for Square 1. Sew left-hand edge of Square 4 to BO edge of Square 1.

SQUARES 5-10
Work as for Square 2, picking up sts for each Square from the previous Square, and sewing Squares 6, 8, and 10 to Squares 3, 5, and 7, respectively, as indicated in Assembly Diagram.

STRIPS 2 AND 3
Work as for Strip 1.

FINISHING
Sew Strips together according to Assembly Diagram.

Block lightly (see Special Techniques, page 156).

CABLE PATTERN

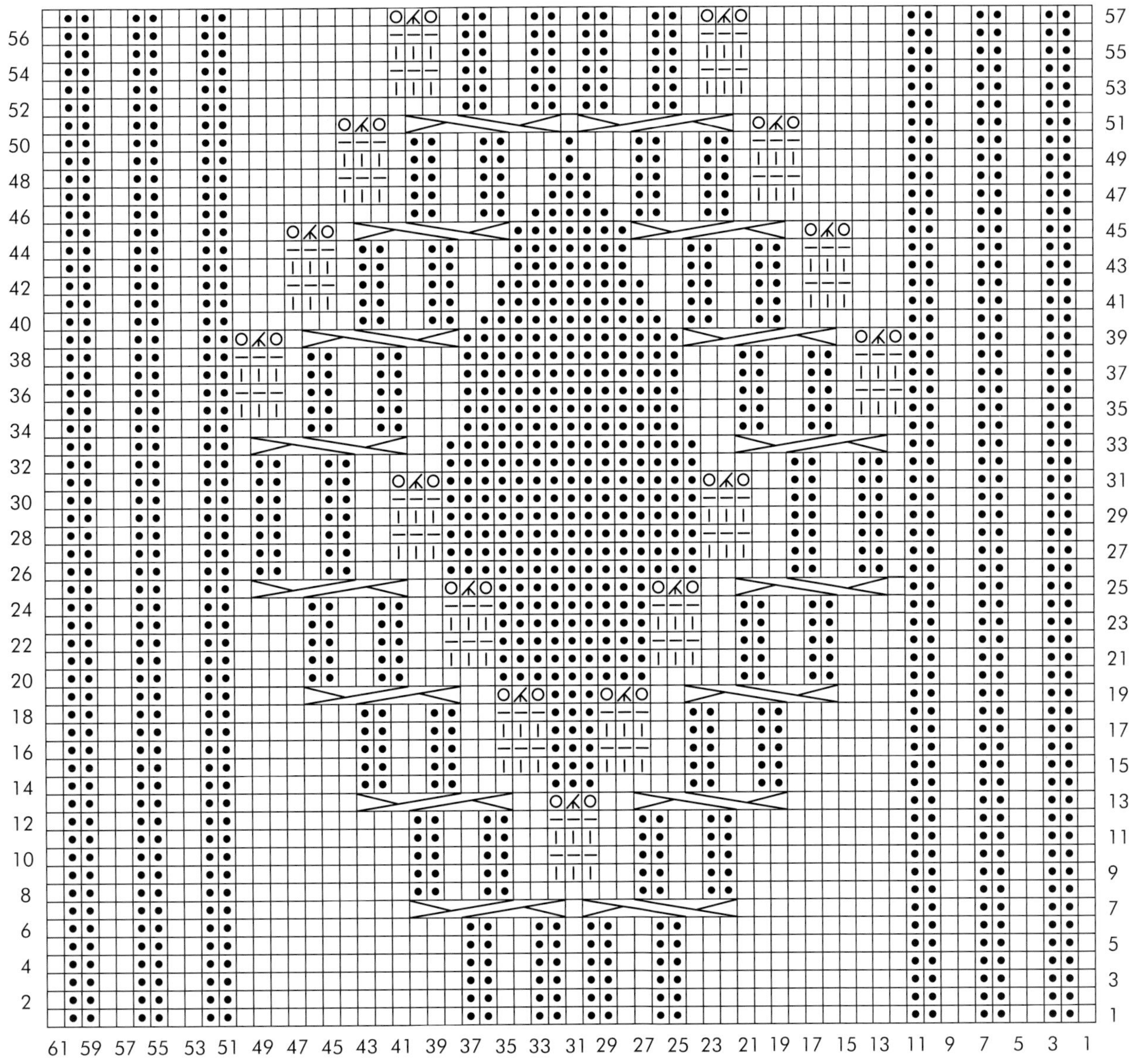

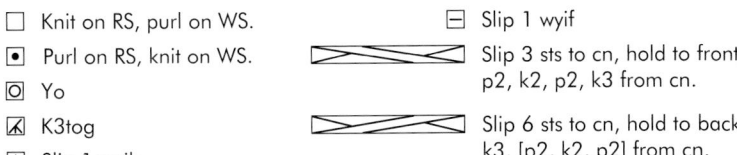

KEY

	Knit on RS, purl on WS.		Slip 1 wyif
□	Knit on RS, purl on WS.	⊟	Slip 1 wyif
⊡	Purl on RS, knit on WS.		Slip 3 sts to cn, hold to front, p2, k2, p2, k3 from cn.
⊙	Yo		
⊠	K3tog		Slip 6 sts to cn, hold to back, k3, [p2, k2, p2] from cn.
Ⅰ	Slip 1 wyib		

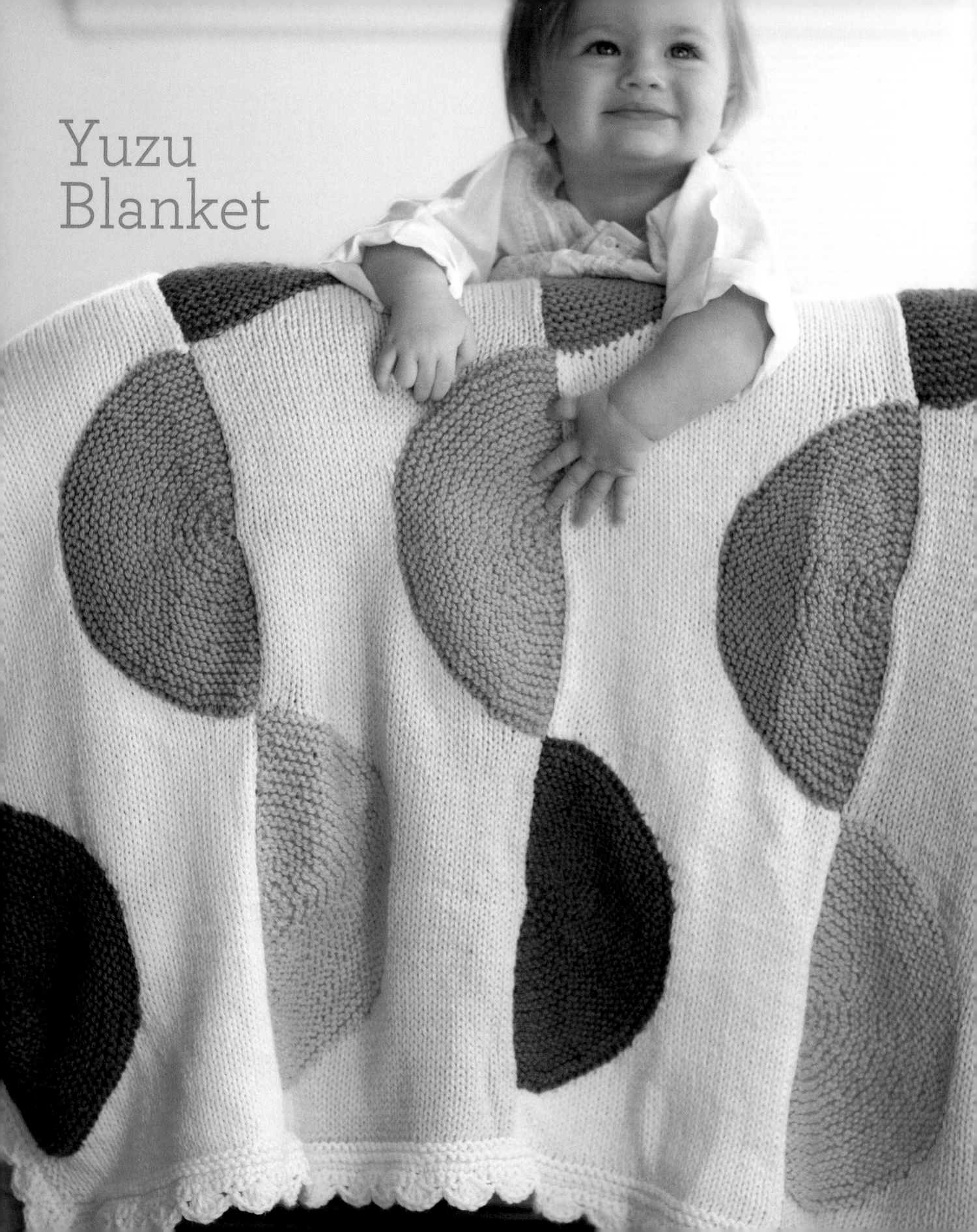

Yuzu
Blanket

To create this eye-catching blanket, vibrant knitted semicircles are stitched into light-colored strips of Stockinette stitch. An edging of cluster-stitch crochet echoes the arcs of the semicircles.

FINISHED MEASUREMENTS
35" wide x 44" long

YARN
Berroco Vintage (50% acrylic / 40% wool / 10% nylon; 100 grams / 217 yards): 3 hanks #5111 Limone (A); 2 hanks #5112 Minty (B); 1 hank each #51180 Grapefruit (C), #5125 Aquae (D), #5175 Fennel (E), #5156 Cork (F), and #51179 Apricot (G)

NEEDLES
One pair straight needles size US 8 (5 mm)
Change needle size if necessary to obtain correct gauge.

CROCHET HOOKS
Crochet hook size H/8 (5 mm)

GAUGE
18 sts and 24 rows = 4" (10 cm) in Stockinette stitch (St st)
18 sts and 34 rows = 4" (10 cm) in Garter stitch (knit every row)

STITCH PATTERN
SHELL EDGING (multple of 4 sts + 1)
Row 1: Ch 1, 1 sc in each st around, turn.
Row 2: Ch 1, skip first sc, 1 sc in each sc to end, ending 1 sc in beginning ch-1, turn.
Row 3: Ch 1, skip first sc, *skip 1 sc, 5 dc in next sc, skip 1 sc, sc in next sc; repeat from * to end, ending 1 sc in beginning ch-1.

STRIPS 1 AND 3
Using B, CO 36 sts. Begin St st; work even for 7 rows.
*__Decrease Row 1 (WS):__ Working at beginning of WS rows, BO 4 sts once, 2 sts 6 times, then 1 st twice—18 sts remain. Work even for 12 rows.
Increase Row 1 (RS): Working at end of RS rows, CO 1 st twice, 2 sts 6 times, then 4 sts once—36 sts. Work even for 1 row. **
Decrease Row 2 (RS): Working at beginning of RS rows, BO 4 sts once, 2 sts 6 times, then 1 st twice—18 sts remain. Work even for 12 rows.
Increase Row 2 (WS): Working at end of WS rows, CO 1 st twice, 2 sts 6 times, then 4 sts once—36 sts. Work even for 1 row. Repeat from * once, then from * to ** once. Work even for 6 rows. BO all sts.

ASSEMBLY DIAGRAM

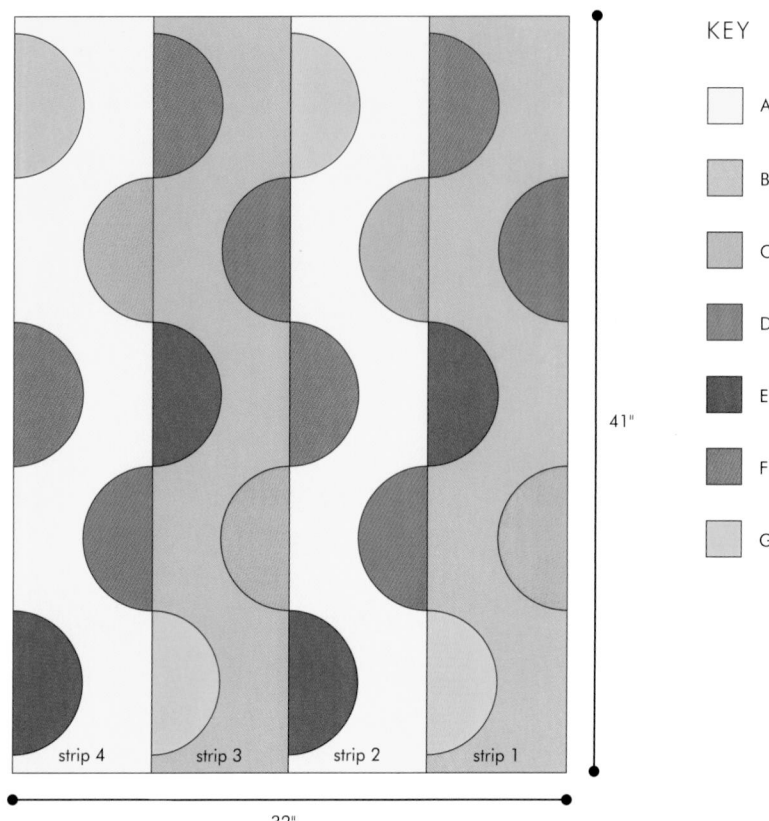

KEY

A

B

C

D

E

F

G

41"

strip 4   strip 3   strip 2   strip 1

32"

STRIPS 2 AND 4
Using A, work as for Strip 1.

HALF CIRCLES (make 4 each in C, D, E, F, and G)
CO 56 sts. Begin Garter st (knit every row); work even for 5 rows.

Decrease Row 1 (RS): K2, *k2tog, k4; repeat from * to end—47 sts remain. Knit 7 rows.

Decrease Row 2: K1, *k2tog, k3; repeat from * to last st, k1—38 sts remain. Knit 7 rows.

Decrease Row 3: K2, *k2tog, k2; repeat from * to end—29 sts remain. Knit 5 rows.

Decrease Row 4: K1, *k2tog, k1; repeat from * to last st, k1—20 sts remain. Knit 3 rows.

Decrease Row 5: K2, *k2tog; repeat from * to end—11 sts remain. Knit 1 row.

Decrease Row 6: *K2tog; repeat from * to last st, k1—6 sts. Cut yarn, leaving an 8" tail; thread through remaining sts, pull tight, and fasten off.

FINISHING
Sew Half Circles into Strips, then sew Strips together, following Assembly Diagram.

Side Edging: Using A, pick up and knit 180 sts evenly along one long side edge. Knit 3 rows. BO all sts knitwise. Repeat for opposite side.

Top and Bottom Edging: Using A, pick up and knit 140 sts evenly along top edge. Knit 3 rows. BO all sts knitwise. Repeat for opposite edge.

Blanket Edging: Using crochet hook, join yarn to any corner of Blanket. Work Shell Edging around entire Blanket.

Block lightly (see Special Techniques, page 156).

Clementine Jumper

Simple and modern, this cross-back jumper is knit in one piece and sewn at the shoulders. The contrasting trim highlights the back shaping (see photo on page 93), while a sprinkling of citrus-colored buttons adorn the front bodice.

SIZES
3 (6, 9, 12, 18, 24) months

FINISHED MEASUREMENTS
19 (20, 22½, 24½, 26½, 30½)" chest

YARN
Berroco Vintage Chunky (50% acrylic / 40% wool / 10% nylon; 100 grams / 130 yards): 2 (2, 2, 2, 3, 3) hanks #6164 Tang (MC); 1 hank #6110 Fondant (A)

NEEDLES
One pair straight needles size US 10½ (6.5 mm)
Change needle size if necessary to obtain correct gauge.

NOTIONS
Stitch holders; nine decorative buttons

GAUGE
14 sts and 21 rows = 4" (10 cm) in Stockinette stitch (St st)

NOTES
Clementine is worked in one piece to the armholes, then the Front and Backs are worked separately to the shoulders. The Back shoulders are crossed and sewn to the opposite Front shoulders.

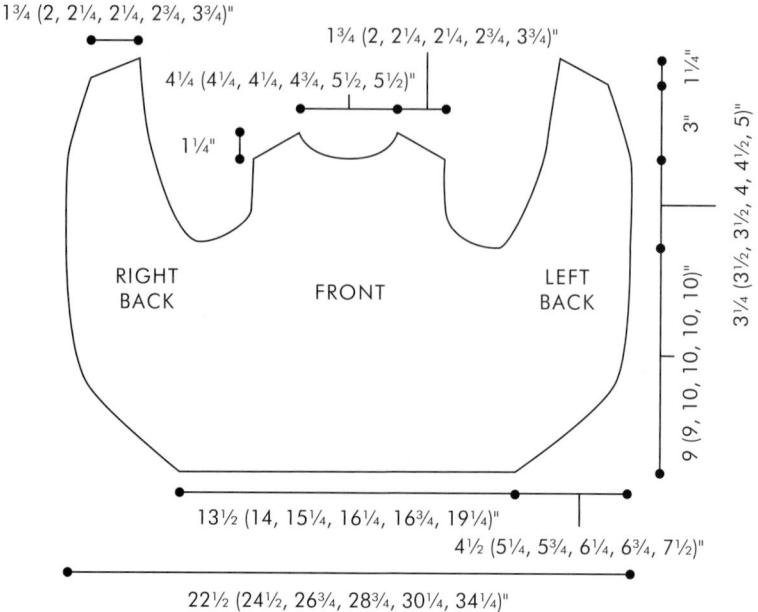

1¾ (2, 2¼, 2¼, 2¾, 3¾)"

1¾ (2, 2¼, 2¼, 2¾, 3¾)"

4¼ (4¼, 4¼, 4¾, 5½, 5½)"

1¼"

1¼"

3"

3¼ (3½, 3½, 4, 4½, 5)"

RIGHT BACK

FRONT

LEFT BACK

9 (9, 10, 10, 10, 10)"

13½ (14, 15¼, 16¼, 16¾, 19¼)"

4½ (5¼, 5¾, 6¼, 6¾, 7½)"

22½ (24½, 26¾, 28¾, 30¼, 34¼)"

BODY

Using MC, CO 47 (49, 53, 57, 59, 67) sts. Purl 1 row.

SHAPE BODY

Next Row (RS): Begin St st. CO 3 sts at beginning of next 2 rows, 2 sts at beginning of next 2 (4, 6, 8, 10, 12) rows, then increase 1 st each side every other row 7 times, then every 4 rows 4 times, as follows: K1, M1, work to last st, M1, k1— 79 (85, 93, 101, 107, 119) sts. Work even until piece measures 9 (9, 10, 10, 10, 10)" from the beginning, ending with a WS row. Place first and last 23 (25, 27, 29, 31, 33) sts on st holders for Backs—33 (35, 39, 43, 45, 53) sts remain for Front.

FRONT

With RS facing, rejoin yarn to Front sts.

SHAPE ARMHOLES

Next Row (RS): BO 2 (2, 2, 2, 2, 3) sts at beginning of next 2 rows, then decrease 1 st each side every other row 1 (1, 2, 2, 1, 3) time(s), as follows: K1, k2tog, work to last 3 sts, ssk, k1— 27 (29, 31, 35, 39, 41) sts remain. Work even until armholes measure 3¼ (3½, 3½, 4, 4½, 5)", ending with a WS row.

SHAPE NECK AND SHOULDERS

Next Row (RS): Work 9 (10, 11, 12, 13, 14) sts, join a second ball of yarn, BO center 9 (9, 9, 11, 13, 13) sts, and work to end. Working both sides at the same time, BO 2 (3, 3, 3, 4, 4) sts at each shoulder edge 3 (1, 2, 3, 1, 2) time(s), then 0 (2, 2, 0, 3, 3) sts 0 (2, 1, 0, 2, 1) time(s) and, AT THE SAME TIME, BO 2 sts at each neck edge once, then 1 st once.

RIGHT BACK

With RS facing, transfer Right Back sts to needle. Rejoin yarn.

SHAPE ARMHOLE

Next Row (RS): BO 2 (2, 3, 3, 3, 3) sts at armhole edge once, decrease 1 st at armhole edge every row 6 times, then every other row 5 (6, 6, 7, 8, 9) times, as follows: On RS rows, k1, ssk, work to end; on WS rows, work to last 3 sts, p2tog, p1—10 (11, 12, 13, 14, 15) sts remain. Work even until armhole measures 3¼ (3½, 3½, 4, 4½, 5)", ending with a WS row.

SHAPE NECK

Next Row (RS): Decrease 1 st at neck edge this row, then every 4 rows 3 times, as follows: Work to last 3 sts, ssk, k1—6 (7, 8, 9, 10, 11) sts remain. Work even until armhole measures 6¼ (6½, 6½, 7, 7½, 8)", ending with a RS row.

SHAPE SHOULDER

Next Row (WS): BO 2 (3, 3, 3, 4, 4) sts at neck edge 3 (1, 2, 3, 1, 2) time(s), then 0 (2, 2, 0, 3, 3) sts 0 (2, 1, 0, 2, 1) time(s).

LEFT BACK

Work as for Right Back, reversing all shaping.

FINISHING

Body Edging: With RS facing, using A, beginning at beginning of Right Back shoulder shaping, pick up and knit 208 (212, 216, 222, 228, 234) sts around entire outside edge, ending at beginning of Left Back shoulder shaping. Knit 2 rows. BO all sts knitwise.

Armhole Edging: With RS facing, using A, beginning at point of Left Back shoulder and ending at beginning of Left Front shoulder shaping, pick up and knit 58 (62, 62, 66, 70, 74) sts along armhole edge. Knit 2 rows. BO all sts knitwise. Repeat for right armhole.

Front Neck Edging: With RS facing, using A, pick up and knit 21 (21, 21, 23, 25, 25) sts across Front neck. Knit 2 rows. BO all sts knitwise.

Sew Left Back shoulder to Right Front shoulder. Sew Right Back shoulder to Left Front shoulder. Sew decorative buttons to Front (see photo on page 91).

Ronald
"Snowsuit"

In the 1930s, all-in-one snowsuits were a popular way to keep kids warm while they tromped around outside. Our version is perfect for romping around indoors and features a belt—a popular design element in children's wear back then—as well as contrasting elbow and knee patches for both practicality and style.

SIZES
3 (6, 9, 12) months

FINISHED MEASUREMENTS
18¾ (19½, 21¼, 23)" chest

YARN
Berroco Vintage (50% acrylic / 40% wool / 10% nylon / 100 grams / 217 yards): 2 (2, 2, 2) hanks #5192 Chana Dal (MC); 1 (1, 2, 2) hanks #5104 Mushroom (A)

NEEDLES
One pair straight needles size US 8 (5 mm)
One pair straight needles size US 6 (4 mm)
One 16" (40 cm) long circular (circ) needle size US 8 (5 mm)
One set of five double-pointed needles (dpn) size US 8 (5 mm)
One set of five double-pointed needles size US 6 (4 mm)
Change needle size if necessary to obtain correct gauge.

NOTIONS
Stitch holders; stitch marker; nine ½" buttons; two ¾" buttons; sewing needle and matching thread

GAUGE
18 sts and 24 rows = 4" (10 cm) in Stockinette stitch (St st), using larger needles

STITCH PATTERNS
1X1 RIB (worked flat) (odd number of sts; 1-row repeat)
Row 1 (RS): K1, *p1, k1; repeat from * to end.
Row 2: Knit the knit sts and purl the purl sts as they face you. Repeat Row 2 for 1x1 Rib.

1X1 RIB (worked in the rnd) (even number of sts; 1-rnd repeat)
All Rnds: *K1, p1; repeat from * to end.

SEED STITCH (odd number of sts; 1-row repeat)
All Rows: K1, *p1, k1; repeat from * to end.

NOTES
Legs are worked back and forth, then joined together in the rnd to begin the Body. The Body is worked in the rnd to the underarms, then divided for Back and Front. Sleeves are picked up from the Body and worked in the rnd to the cuffs.

LEGS
With smaller straight needles and MC, CO 29 (31, 31, 35) sts. Begin 1x1 Rib (worked flat); work even until piece measures 1", ending with a RS row.
Next Row (WS): Change to larger needles; purl 1 row, decreasing 5 (5, 3, 5) sts evenly—24 (26, 28, 30) sts remain.

BODY

With RS facing, transfer first 21 (22, 24, 26) sts from first Leg to right-hand end of larger circ needle. Using MC, knit across last 21 (22, 24, 26) sts of first Leg, 42 (44, 48, 52) sts from second Leg, then first 21 (22, 24, 26) sts of first Leg—84 (88, 96, 104) sts. Join for working in the rnd; pm for beginning of rnd. Continuing in St st, work even until piece measures 10½" from beginning of Body.

DIVIDE FOR BACK AND FRONT
Next Rnd: Change to A; k42 (44, 48, 52), transfer next 42 (44, 48, 52) sts to st holder for Front.

BACK

Next Row (WS): Continuing in St st, work even for 3¾ (4, 4¼, 4½)", ending with a WS row. BO all sts.

FRONT

Next Row (RS): Rejoin yarn to sts on holder for Front. Continuing in St st, work even for 2¼ (2½, 2¾, 3)", ending with a WS row.

SHAPE FRONT NECK
Next Row (RS): K13 (14, 16, 17), join a second ball of yarn, BO center 16 (16, 16, 18) sts, knit to end. Working both sides at the same time, decrease 1 st at each neck edge every other row 4 times—9 (10, 12, 13) sts remain each side. Work even until piece measures same as for Back. BO all sts. Sew shoulder seams.

SLEEVES

With RS facing, using larger dpns and A, beginning at bottom center of underarm, pick up and knit 34 (36, 38, 40) sts around armhole. Divide sts among dpns. Join for working in the rnd; pm for beginning of rnd. Begin St st; work even for 1".

SHAPE SLEEVE
Next Rnd: Decrease 2 sts this rnd, every 6 rnds 1 (1, 5, 5) time(s), then every 8 rnds 3 (3, 0, 0) times, as follows: K1, k2tog, knit to last 3 sts, ssk, k1—24 (26, 26, 28) sts remain. Work even until piece measures 6½" from pick-up rnd.
Next Rnd: Change to smaller needles. Knit 1 rnd, increasing 4 sts evenly spaced—28 (30, 30, 32) sts.
Next Rnd: Change to 1x1 Rib (worked in the rnd); work even for 1". BO all sts in pattern.

SHAPE LEG

Next Row (RS): Continuing in St st, increase 1 st each side this row, every other row 5 (6, 7, 8) times, then every row 12 (11, 11, 11) times, as follows: Work 1 st, M1, work to last st, M1, work 1 st—60 (62, 66, 70) sts. Work even until piece measures 5 (5½, 6, 6)" from the beginning, ending with a WS row.

SHAPE CROTCH

Next Row (RS): BO 2 sts at beginning of next 8 rows, then 1 st at beginning of next 2 rows—42 (44, 48, 52) sts remain. Transfer sts to st holder for first Leg; leave on the needle for second Leg.

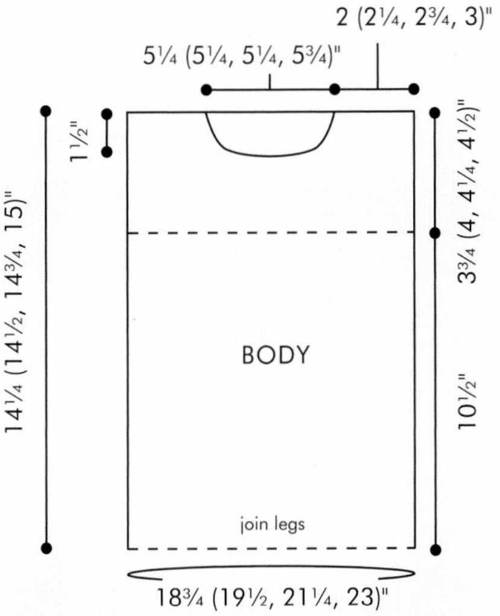
2 (2¼, 2¾, 3)"
5¼ (5¼, 5¼, 5¾)"
1½"
14¼ (14½, 14¾, 15)"
3¾ (4, 4¼, 4½)"
BODY
10½"
join legs
18¾ (19½, 21¼, 23)"

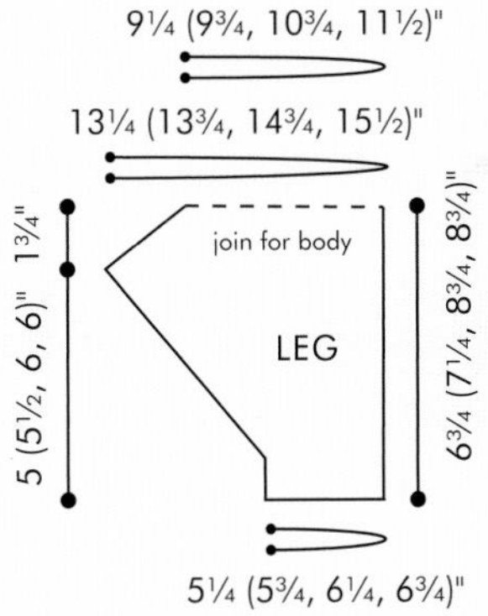
9¼ (9¾, 10¾, 11½)"
13¼ (13¾, 14¾, 15½)"
1¾"
join for body
6¾ (7¼, 8¾, 8¾)"
LEG
5 (5½, 6, 6)"
5¼ (5¾, 6¼, 6¾)"

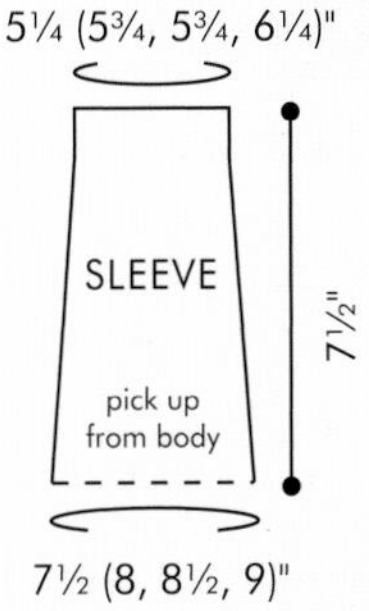
5¼ (5¾, 5¾, 6¼)"
SLEEVE
7½"
pick up
from body
7½ (8, 8½, 9)"

KNEE PATCHES

Using larger straight needles and A, CO 9 sts.

SHAPE KNEE PATCH

Next Row: Begin Seed st; increase 1 st each side this row, then every other row twice, working increased sts in Seed st as they become available—15 sts. Work even until piece measures 2" from the beginning, ending with a WS row.

Next Row: Decrease 1 st each side this row, then every other row twice—9 sts remain. BO all sts.

ELBOW PATCHES

Using MC, work as for Knee Patches.

FINISHING

Leg Button Band: Using larger straight needles and MC, CO 5 sts. Begin 1x1 Rib (worked flat); work even until Band, slightly stretched, is long enough to fit from lower edge of back half of left Leg, through crotch, to lower edge of back half of Right Leg. Sew in place. Mark placement of 9 buttons, one each at center of cuff at front and back, one at center of crotch, and the remaining 6 evenly spaced between.

Leg Buttonhole Band: Work as for Button Band to first marker, ending with a WS row.

Buttonhole Row (RS): Work 2 sts, yo, k2tog, k1. Complete as for Button Band, working remaining 8 buttonholes opposite markers.

Sew Buttonhole Band in place.

Sew ½" buttons at markers.

Neckband: Using smaller dpns and A, pick up and knit 60 (60, 60, 64) sts evenly around neckline. Divide sts evenly among dpns. Join for working in the rnd; pm for beginning of rnd. Begin 1x1 Rib (worked in the rnd); work even for 5 rnds. BO all sts in pattern.

Belt: Using smaller straight needles and A, CO 11 sts. Begin 1x1 Rib (worked flat); work even until piece measures 19 (20, 22, 23½)" from the beginning, ending with a RS row.

Buttonhole Row (WS): Work 5 sts, yo, k2tog, work to end. Work even for 1", ending with a RS row. Repeat Buttonhole Row. Work even for ½". BO all sts in pattern. Sew ¾" buttons at end opposite buttonholes.

Using sewing needle and thread, lightly tack Belt to Body along Back. Lightly tack first 2" of button end of Belt to center Front. Sew Elbow Patch to each Sleeve. Sew Knee Patch to each Leg.

Diamond
Bunting

This classic baby bunting is an easy way to keep your little one warm on a chilly day. The bold stitch pattern is borrowed from adult fisherman sweaters of Ireland, and the yarn color is meant to mimic the natural, uncolored shade of wool that is often used in traditional Irish sweaters.

SIZES
One size

FINISHED MEASUREMENTS
24" chest

YARN
Berroco Vintage DK (50% acrylic / 40% wool / 10% nylon; 100 grams / 288 yards): 4 hanks #2105 Oats

NEEDLES
One pair straight needles size US 7 (4.5 mm)
One pair straight needles size US 6 (4 mm)
Change needle size if necessary to obtain correct gauge.

NOTIONS
Stitch markers; stitch holders; cable needle (cn); six ⅝" buttons

GAUGE
22 sts and 30 rows = 4" (10 cm) in Moss stitch, using larger needles

STITCH PATTERN
MOSS STITCH (any number of sts; 4-row repeat)
Row 1 (RS): *K1, p1; repeat from * to end, end k1 if an odd number of sts.
Row 2: Knit the knit sts and purl the purl sts as they face you.
Row 3: Purl the knit sts and knit the purl sts as they face you.
Row 4: Repeat Row 2.
Repeat Rows 1-4 for Moss st.

BACK
Using larger needles, CO 73 sts. Begin Moss st; work even until piece measures 3" from the beginning, ending with a RS row.
Increase Row (WS): Change to smaller needles. Work 3 sts in Moss st, increase 9 sts over next 30 sts, work 6 sts in Moss st, increase 10 sts over next 31 sts, work in Moss st to end—92 sts.
Next Row: Work 3 sts in Moss st, work *Chart 1 over 5 sts, Chart 2 over 30 sts, then Chart 3 over 5 sts**, pm, work Moss st over next 6 sts, pm, repeat from * to ** once, pm, work in Moss st to end. Work even until piece measures 8" from the beginning, ending with a WS row.

SHAPE SIDES
Next Row (RS): Decrease 1 st each side this row, then every 4½" twice—86 sts remain. Work even until piece measures 20" from the beginning, ending with a WS row.

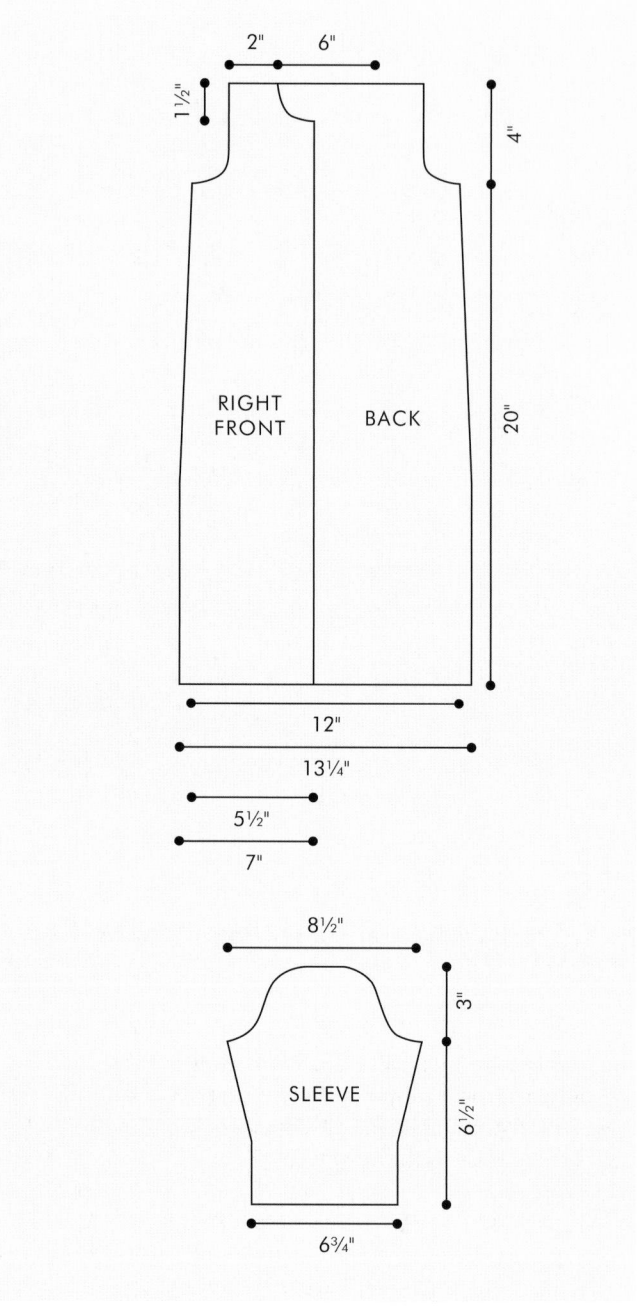

SHAPE ARMHOLES

Next Row (RS): BO 3 sts at beginning of next 2 rows, decrease 1 st each side every row 6 times, then every other row twice—64 sts remain. Work even until armhole measures 4", ending with a WS row. BO all sts.

RIGHT FRONT

Using larger needles, CO 39 sts. Begin Moss st; work even until piece measures 3" from the beginning, ending with a RS row.

Next Row (WS): Change to smaller needles. Work 3 sts in Moss st, working increases into Moss st, increase 10 sts evenly across to last 6 sts, work in Moss st to end—49 sts.

Next Row: Work 6 sts in Moss st and transfer to st holder for Front Band, work Chart 1 over 5 sts, Chart 2 over 30 sts, then Chart 3 over 5 sts, pm, work in Moss st to end—43 sts. Work even until piece measures 8" from the beginning, ending with a WS row.

SHAPE SIDES

Next Row (RS): Decrease 1 st at side edge this row, then every 4½" twice—40 sts. Work even until piece measures 20" from the beginning, ending with a RS row.

SHAPE ARMHOLE

Next Row (WS): BO 3 sts at armhole edge once, decrease 1 st at armhole edge every row 6 times, then every other row twice—29 sts remain. Work even until armhole measures 2½", ending with a WS row.

SHAPE NECK

Next Row (RS): BO 8 sts at neck edge once, then decrease 1 st at neck edge every row 9 times—12 sts remain. Work even until armhole measures 4", ending with a WS row. BO all sts.

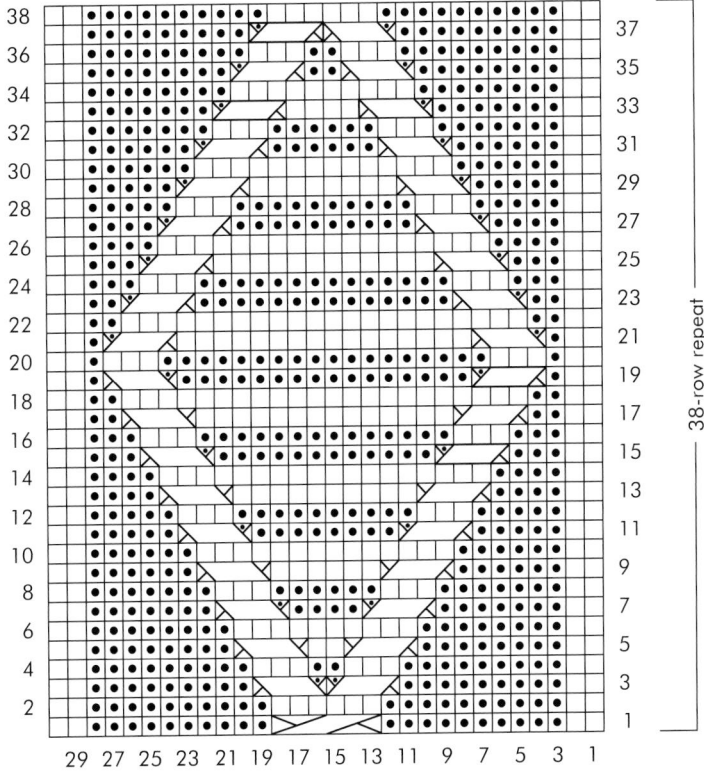

CHART 2

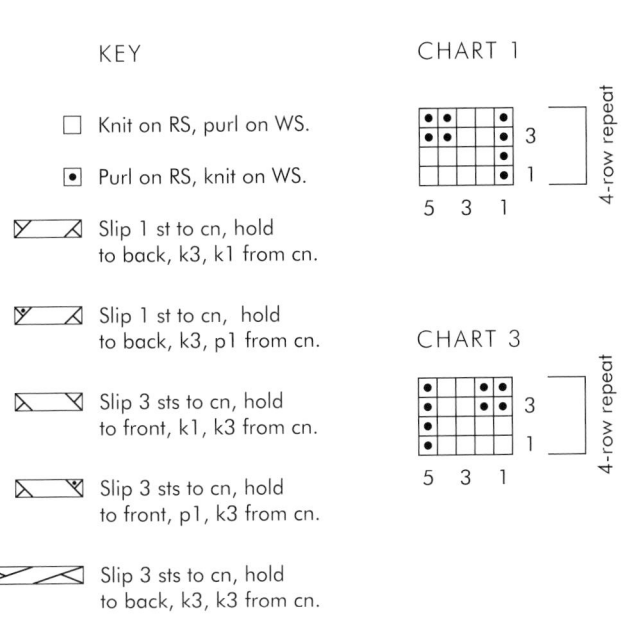

KEY

☐ Knit on RS, purl on WS.

⊡ Purl on RS, knit on WS.

Slip 1 st to cn, hold
to back, k3, k1 from cn.

Slip 1 st to cn, hold
to back, k3, p1 from cn.

Slip 3 sts to cn, hold
to front, k1, k3 from cn.

Slip 3 sts to cn, hold
to front, p1, k3 from cn.

Slip 3 sts to cn, hold
to back, k3, k3 from cn.

CHART 1

4-row repeat

3

1

5 3 1

CHART 3

4-row repeat

3

1

5 3 1

LEFT FRONT

Work as for Right Front, reversing all pattern placements and
shaping.

SLEEVES

Using larger needles, CO 37 sts. Begin Moss st; work even until
piece measures 2½" from the beginning, ending with a RS row.
Next row (WS): Work 3 sts in Moss st, working increases into
Moss st, increase 9 sts evenly to last 3 sts, work in Moss st to
end—46 sts.
Next Row: Change to smaller needles. Work 3 sts in Moss st,
work Chart 1 over 5 sts, Chart 2 over 30 sts, then Chart 3 over 5
sts, work in Moss st to end. Work even for 1 row.

SHAPE SLEEVE
Next Row (RS): Increase 1 st each side this row, then every
4 rows 5 times, as follows: K1, M1, work to last st, M1, k1—58
sts. Working increased sts in Moss st as they become available,
work even until piece measures 6½" from the beginning, ending with a WS row.

SHAPE CAP
Next Row (RS): BO 3 sts at beginning of next 2 rows, decrease
1 st each side every other row 6 times, then every row 8 times,
then BO 5 sts at beginning of next 2 rows. BO remaining 14 sts.

FINISHING

Sew shoulder seams. Set in Sleeves; sew side and Sleeve
seams. Sew CO edges of Front and Back together.

Button Band: With RS facing, using larger needles, work
across 6 sts from st holder for Left Front, CO 1 st between
Band and Front—7 sts. Work even in Moss st until Band,
slightly stretched, reaches beginning of neck shaping. BO all
sts. Sew in place. Place markers for 6 buttons on Left Front,
the first ½" above Moss st bottom band, the last ½" below Front
neck shaping, and the remaining 4 evenly spaced between.

Buttonhole Band: Work as for Button Band, working buttonholes opposite markers as follows: (RS) Work 3 sts, yo, k2tog,
work to end.

Collar: With larger needles, CO 85 sts. Begin Moss st; work
even for 3". BO all sts. Sew CO edge of Collar to neck edge.
Sew buttons to Left Front at markers.

Terra
Blanket

This blanket shares its traditional cabled diamond motif with the bunting on page 99. Four long columns of diamonds intersect with a single perpendicular row of diamonds. The result feels both classic and modern.

FINISHED MEASUREMENTS
36" wide x 42" long

YARN
Berroco Vintage (50% acrylic / 40% wool / 10% nylon; 100 grams / 217 yards): 7 hanks #5103 Mocha

NEEDLES
One 29" (70 cm) long or longer circular (circ) needle size US 8 (5 mm)
One 29" (70 cm) long or longer circular needle size US 7 (4.5 mm)
Change needle size if necessary to obtain correct gauge.

NOTIONS
Cable needle (cn)

GAUGE
24 sts and 24 rows = 4" (10 cm) in Cable Pattern from Chart, using larger needle

STITCH PATTERN
MOSS STITCH (even number of sts; 4-row repeat)
Row 1: *K1, p1; repeat from * to end.
Row 2: Knit the knit sts and purl the purl sts as they face you.
Row 3: Purl the knit sts and knit the purl sts as they face you.
Row 4: Repeat Row 2.
Repeat Rows 1-4 for Moss st.

AFGHAN
BASE STRIP
Using larger needles, CO 42 sts.
Row 1 (RS): K1 (edge st, keep in St st), work Chart 1 over 5 sts, Chart 2 over 30 sts, then Chart 3 over 5 sts, k1 (edge st, keep in St st). Working first and last st in St st, work even until 4 vertical repeats of Cable Pattern have been completed, then work Rows 1-4 once. BO all sts.

MAIN STRIP
With RS of Base Strip facing, using larger needle, pick up and knit 174 sts along right-hand edge of Base Strip. Knit 1 row.
Row 1 (RS): K1 (edge st, keep in St st), work **Chart 1 over 5 sts, Chart 2 over 30 sts, then Chart 3 over 5 sts**, *work Moss st over 4 sts; repeat from ** to ** once; repeat from * to last st, k1 (edge st; keep in St st).
Working first and last st in St st, work even until 4 vertical repeats of Cable Pattern have been completed, then work Rows 1-4 once. BO all sts in pattern.

CHART 1

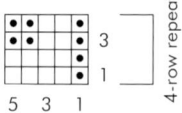

4-row repeat
3
1
5 3 1

CHART 3

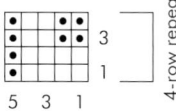

4-row repeat
3
1
5 3 1

CHART 2

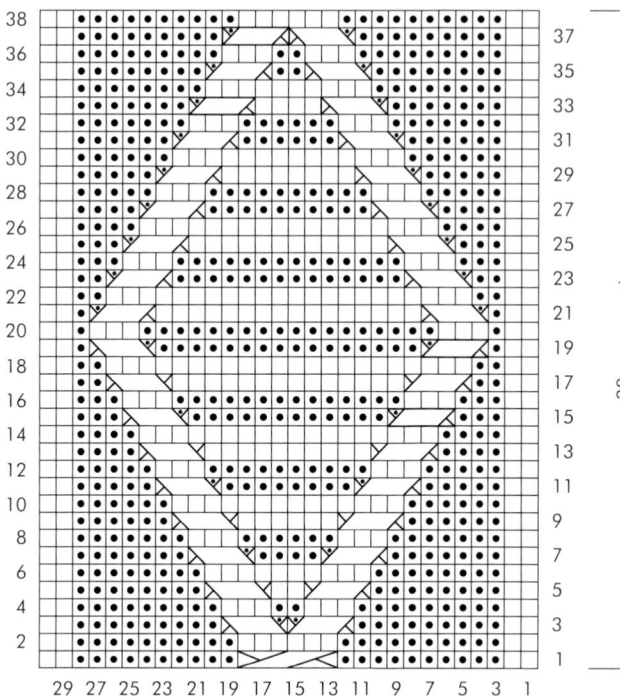

38 36 34 32 30 28 26 24 22 20 18 16 14 12 10 8 6 4 2

37 35 33 31 29 27 25 23 21 19 17 15 13 11 9 7 5 3 1

38-row repeat

29 27 25 23 21 19 17 15 13 11 9 7 5 3 1

KEY

⊡ Purl on RS, knit on WS.

Slip 1 st to cn, hold to back, k3, k1 from cn.

Slip 1 st to cn, hold to back, k3, p1 from cn.

Slip 3 sts to cn, hold to front, k1, k3 from cn.

Slip 3 sts to cn, hold to front, p1, k3 from cn.

Slip 3 sts to cn, hold to back, k3, k3 from cn.

FINISHING

Side Edgings: With RS of Afghan facing, using smaller needle, pick up and knit 162 sts along right-hand edge of Main Strip and Base Strip. Begin Moss st; work even for 4". BO all sts in pattern. Repeat for opposite edge, beginning at Base Strip.

Top Edging: With RS of Afghan facing, using smaller needle, pick up and knit 172 sts along BO edge of Main Strip and Side Edgings. Begin Moss st; work even for 4". BO all sts in pattern.

Bottom Edging: With RS of Afghan facing, using smaller needle, pick up and knit 172 sts along left-hand edge of Base Strip and Side Edgings. Begin Moss st; work even for 4". BO all sts in pattern.

Block lightly (see Special Techniques, page 156).

Calico Blanket

This simple stranded colorwork blanket takes its inspiration from American calico patchwork quilts. The same easy pattern is repeated for each square, with all three colors taking a turn as the background. For ease of knitting, we constructed it in strips and then sewed the strips together, but an experienced knitter might want to take it one step further and work the blanket all at once, using intarsia for the color changes.

FINISHED MEASUREMENTS
Blanket: 37" wide x 43" long
Strip: 6" wide x 42" long

YARN
Berroco Comfort (50% super fine nylon / 50% super fine acrylic; 100 grams / 210 yards): 4 skeins #9749 Aunt Abby Rose (A); 3 skeins each #9705 Pretty Pink (B) and #9727 Spanish Brown (C)

NEEDLES
One pair straight needles size US 9 (5.5 mm)
One 29" (70 cm) long or longer circular (circ) needle size US 9 (5.5 mm)
Change needle size if necessary to obtain correct gauge.

GAUGE
18 sts and 24 rows = 4" (10 cm) in Stockinette stitch (St st)

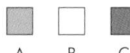

KEY

A
B
C

CHART 1

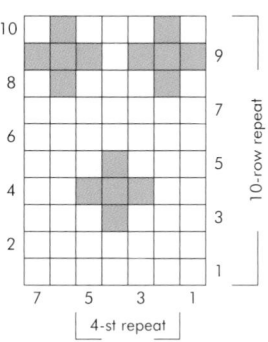

10
9
8
7
6
5
4
3
2
1
7 5 3 1
10-row repeat
4-st repeat

CHART 2

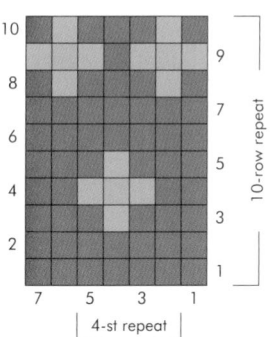

10
9
8
7
6
5
4
3
2
1
7 5 3 1
10-row repeat
4-st repeat

CHART 3

6
5
4
3
2
1
7 5 3 1
6-row repeat
4-st repeat

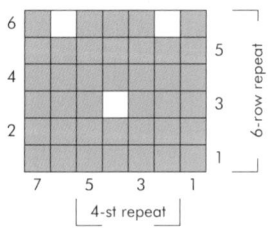

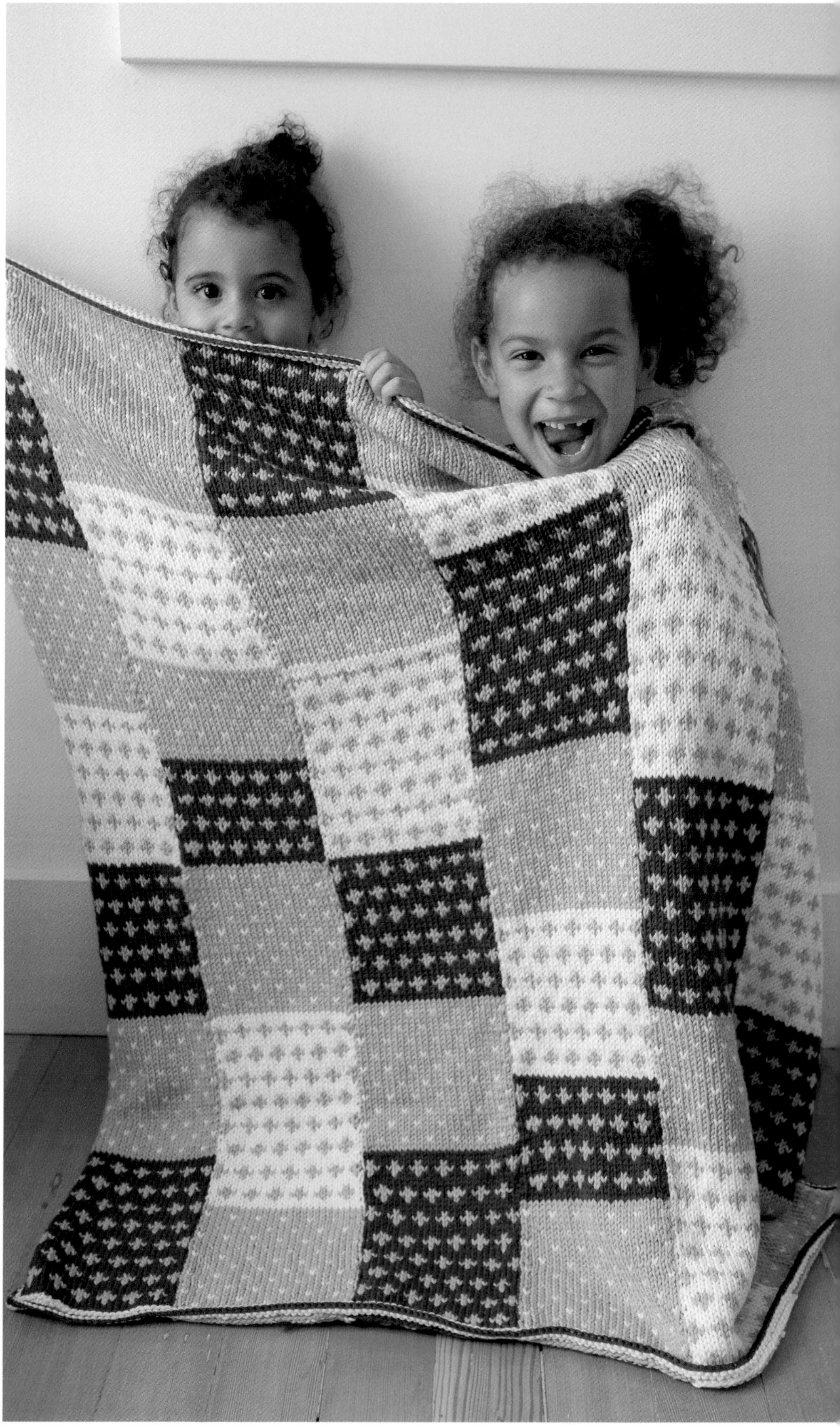

BLANKET

For all Strips, CO 27 sts using color indicated in Row 1 of the first Chart in the Strip. End each Chart section with Row 2, and begin the next Chart section with Row 1.

Strip 1: Work Chart 3 for 8", Chart 2 for 6", Chart 1 for 8", Chart 3 for 6", Chart 2 for 4", Chart 1 for 6", then Chart 3 for 4". BO all sts.

Strip 2: Work Chart 1 for 8", Chart 3 for 6", Chart 2 for 8", Chart 1 for 8", Chart 3 for 6", then Chart 2 for 6". BO all sts.

Strip 3: Work Chart 3 for 6", Chart 2 for 4", Chart 1 for 6", Chart 3 for 8", Chart 2 for 8", Chart 1 for 6", then Chart 3 for 4". BO all sts.

Strip 4: Work Chart 2 for 8", Chart 3 for 6", Chart 2 for 6", Chart 1 for 8", Chart 3 for 6", then Chart 2 for 8". BO all sts.

Strip 5: Work Chart 3 for 6", Chart 1 for 8", Chart 3 for 6", Chart 2 for 4", Chart 3 for 4", Chart 1 for 6", then Chart 3 for 8". BO all sts.

Strip 6: Work Chart 2 for 8", Chart 3 for 6", Chart 2 for 6", Chart 1 for 6", Chart 3 for 6", Chart 2 for 6", then Chart 1 for 4". BO all sts.

FINISHING

Sew all Strips together following Assembly Diagram, sewing through half of the edge st on each Strip to minimize seams.

Side Edging: With RS facing, using circ needle and B, pick up and knit 188 sts along one side edge of Blanket. Knit 3 rows. Change to C; BO all sts. Repeat for opposite edge.

Top and Bottom Edging: With RS facing, using circ needle and B, pick up and knit 166 sts along CO edge of Blanket, including Side Edging. Knit 3 rows. Change to C; BO all sts. Repeat for BO edge.

Block lightly (see Special Techniques, page 156).

ASSEMBLY DIAGRAM

Strip 6   Strip 5   Strip 4   Strip 3   Strip 2   Strip 1

☐ Chart 1

■ Chart 2

▧ Chart 3

Butterfly
Blanket

The clever 1930s patchwork coverlet that inspired this blanket was pieced from old flour sacks and embellished with multicolored butterfly shapes cut from the fabric of old dresses. The squares in our blanket are made of crocheted linen stitch and are embellished with "granny triangles" in variegated shades to replicate the butterflies. In both versions, the butterflies' bodies are outlined in embroidered backstitch, and each square is outlined in running stitch.

FINISHED MEASUREMENTS
Blanket: 32" wide x 40" long
Square: 8" x 8"

YARN
Berroco Comfort (50% super fine nylon / 50% super fine acrylic; 100 grams / 210 yards): 8 skeins #9703 Barley (MC); 1 skein each #9808 Galaxy Mix (A), #9805 Berry Mix (B), #9810 Nosegay Mix (C), and #9727 Spanish Brown (D).

CROCHET HOOKS
Crochet hook size US I/9 (5.5 mm)
Crochet hook size US G/6 (4 mm)
Change hook size if necessary to obtain correct gauge.

NOTIONS
Sewing needle and matching thread, for Butterflies; tapestry needle

GAUGE
20 sts and 20 rows = 4" (10 cm) in Square pattern, using larger hook

ABBREVIATIONS
Dc4tog: Yo, [insert hook into next dc and pull up a loop, yo and pull through 2 loops] 4 times, yo and pull through all 5 loops on hook.
Dc5tog: Yo, [insert hook into next dc and pull up a loop, yo and pull through 2 loops] 5 times, yo and pull through all 6 loops on hook.

KEY

- ▢ MC
- ◼ A
- ◼ B
- ◼ C
- ◼ D (embroidery)
- − running sts
- • French knot

ASSEMBLY DIAGRAM

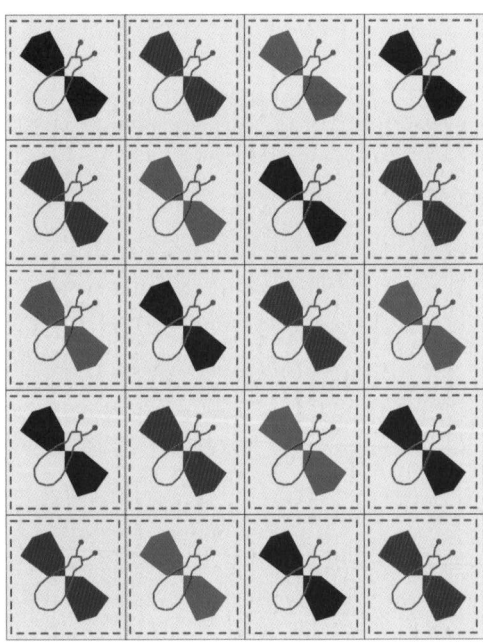

SQUARE (make 20)

Using larger hook and MC, ch 41.

Row 1: Sc in third ch from hook, *ch 1, skip next ch, sc in next ch; repeat from * to end, turn—40 sts remain.

Row 2: Ch 2, sc in next ch-1 sp, *ch 1, skip next sc, sc in next ch-1 sp; repeat from * to end, ending with last sc in top of beginning ch-2, turn.

Repeat Row 2 until Square measures 8" from beginning. Fasten off, leaving a tail long enough to sew Square to next Square.

BUTTERFLY WINGS (make 14 Wings each with A and B and 12 Wings with C)

Using smaller hook, begin with a sliding loop.

Rnd 1: Ch 3 (counts as dc), 4 dc in ring, ch 3, *5 dc in ring, ch 3; repeat from * once, join with a slip st in top of beginning ch-3—3 ch-3 sps.

Rnd 2: Ch 3 (counts as dc), dc4tog across next 4 dc (cluster made), ch 6, sc in next ch-3 sp, ch 6, *dc5tog across next 5 dc, ch 6, sc in next ch-3 sp, ch 6; repeat from * once, join with a slip st in top of first cluster.

Rnd 3: Ch 1, [sc, ch 3, sc] in first cluster, 6 sc in each of next 2 ch-6 sps, *[sc, ch 3, sc] in top of next cluster, 6 sc in each of next 2 ch-6 sps; repeat from * once, join with a slip st in first sc.

Rnd 4: Ch 1, sc in first sc, *[sc, ch 3, sc] in next ch-3 sp, sc in next 14 sc; repeat from * to end, omitting last sc, join with a slip st in first sc. Fasten off.

FINISHING

Place 2 Wings of the same color on any Square with points touching in center. Sew edges of Wings in place with sewing needle and thread. With tapestry needle and D, embroider body, head and antennae of Butterfly using backstitch and following diagram. Make 1 French knot at end of each antenna. Work 1 row of running st around each Square (see Special Techniques, page 156). Sew Squares together following Assembly Diagram.

Edging: With RS facing, join MC in any corner of Blanket, ch 1, working from left to right, reverse sc in each st around Blanket. Join with a slip st in first sc. Fasten off.

Block lightly (see Special Techniques, page 156).

Bertie Bird

The body of our birdie is worked in Stockinette stitch, and the wing tips and tail are worked in feather and fan stitch (how fitting!). Little details like I-cord feet and a bright yellow beak are a fun nod to realism.

FINISHED MEASUREMENTS
10" long x 5" high

YARN
Berroco Vintage Chunky (50% acrylic / 40% wool / 10% nylon; 100 grams / 130 yards): 1 hank each #6105 Oats (A), #6125 Aquae (B), #6179 Chocolate (C), and #6122 Banana (D)

NEEDLES
One pair straight needles size US 9 (5.5 mm)
One pair straight needles size US 10 (6 mm)
One pair double-pointed needles (dpn) size US 5 (3.75 mm)
Change needle size if necessary to obtain correct gauge.

NOTIONS
Sewing needle and thread in matching colors; stuffing; tapestry needle

GAUGE
17 sts and 24 rows = 4" (10 cm) in Stockinette stitch (St st), using size US 9 (5.5 mm) needles

CHEST

Using size US 9 needles and A, CO 3 sts. Begin St st; work even for 2 rows.

SHAPE CHEST

Next Row (RS): Increase 1 st each side this row, then every other row 4 times, as follows: K1, M1, work to last st, M1, k1—13 sts. Work even until piece measures 5" from the beginning, ending with a WS row.

Next Row (RS): Decrease 1 st each side this row, then every other row 4 times, as follows: K2tog, work to last 2 sts, ssk—3 sts remain.

Work even until piece measures 8" from the beginning, ending with a WS row. BO all sts.

RIGHT SIDE

Using size US 9 needles and B, CO 3 sts.

SHAPE RIGHT SIDE

Increase Row 1 (RS): K1, M1, work to end—4 sts.

Increase Row 2 (WS): Purl to last st, M1-p, p1—5 sts.

Repeat Increase Row 1 every other row 8 times—13 sts. Purl 1 row.

SHAPE HEAD AND WING SLIT

Increase Row 3 (RS): Knit to last st, M1, k1—14 sts. Purl 1 row.

Next Row (RS): K4, BO next 5 sts, knit to last st, M1, k1. Purl 1 row, CO 5 sts over BO sts—15 sts.

Increase Row 4 (RS): K1, M1, knit to end—16 sts.

Increase Row 5: Purl to last st, M1-p, p1—17 sts.

SHAPE NECK

Decrease Row 6 (RS): Decrease 1 st at beginning of this row, then every other row twice, as follows: K2tog, knit to end—14 sts remain. Purl 1 row.

Next Row (RS): BO 2 sts at beginning of this row, then 3 sts at beginning of next 2 RS rows and, AT THE SAME TIME, decrease 1 st at end of every RS row 3 times, ending with a RS row—3 sts remain. BO all sts.

LEFT SIDE

Work as for Right Side, reversing all shaping.

TOP HEAD PANEL

Using size US 9 needles and B, CO 1 st.

SHAPE PANEL

Increase Row 1 (RS): K1-f/b— 2 sts.

Increase Row 2: P1, M1-p, p1—3 sts.

Increase Row 3: Increase 1 st each side this row, then every other row once, as follows: K1, M1, knit to last st, M1, k1—7 sts. Work even in St st until piece measures 2" from the beginning, ending with a WS row.

Next Row (RS): Decrease 1 st each side this row, then every 4 rows once, as follows: K2tog, work to last 2 sts, ssk—3 sts remain. Work even until piece measures 3" from the beginning, ending with a WS row. BO all sts.

TAIL

Using size US 9 needles and B, CO 7 sts. Begin St st, beginning with a purl row; work even for 5 rows, knitting first and last st of every row.

Next Row (RS): Increase 1 st each side this row, then every other row 4 times, as follows: K1, M1, work to last st, M1, k1—17 sts. Work even for 1 row.

WORK LACE PATTERN

Row 1 (RS): Change to C. K2, [k2tog] twice, yo, [k1, yo] 5 times, [k2tog] twice, k2—19 sts.

Row 2: Knit.

Row 3: Change to D. K1, [k2tog] 3 times, yo, [k1, yo] 5 times, [k2tog] 3 times, k1.

Row 4: Knit.

Row 5: Change to B. Knit.

Row 6: K1, purl to last st, k1.

Row 7: Repeat Row 3.

Row 8: Knit.

Rows 9 and 10: Change to largest needles and C. Repeat Rows 3 and 4.

Rows 11 and 12: Change to D. Repeat Rows 3 and 4. BO all sts.

TAIL LINING

Using size US 9 needles and A, CO 7 sts.

SHAPE LINING

Next Row (RS): Increase 1 st each side this row, then every other row 5 times, as follows: K1, M1, work to last st, M1, k1—19 sts. Purl 1 row. Work even in St st, knitting first and last st of every row, until piece measures 4½" from the beginning, ending with a WS row.

Next Row (RS): BO 4 sts at beginning of next 2 rows, then 3 sts at beginning of next 2 rows. BO remaining 5 sts.

WINGS (make 2)

Using size US 9 needles and B, CO 7 sts. Begin St st, beginning with a purl row; work even for 5 rows, knitting first and last st of every row.

Increase Row (RS): Increase 1 st each side this row then every other row twice, as follows: K1, M1, work to last st, M1, k1—13 sts. Work even for 1 row.

WORK LACE PATTERN

Row 1 (RS): Change to C. K1, [k2tog] twice, yo, [k1, yo] 3 times, [k2tog] twice, k1.

Row 2: Knit.

Rows 3 and 4: Change to D. Repeat Rows 1 and 2.

Row 5: Change to B. Knit.

Row 6: K1, purl to last st, k1.

Rows 7 and 8: Repeat Rows 1 and 2.

Rows 9 and 10: Change to largest needles and C. Repeat Rows 1 and 2.

Rows 11 and 12: Change to D. Repeat Rows 1 and 2. BO all sts.

WING LINING (make 2)

Using size US 9 needles and A, CO 7 sts. Begin St st, beginning with a purl row; work even for 5 rows, knitting first and last st of every row.

Increase Row (RS): Increase 1 st each side this row, then every other row twice, as follows: K1, M1, work to last st, M1, k1—13 sts. Work even for 1 row.

Next Row (RS): Work even, knitting the first and last st of every row, until piece measures 3" from the beginning, ending with a WS row.

Next Row (RS): BO 3 sts at beginning of next 2 rows, then 2 sts at beginning of next 2 rows. BO remaining 3 sts.

FINISHING

Note: Sew pieces together using sewing needle and thread.
With WSs together, sew Tail and Tail Lining together. With WSs together, sew Wing and Wing Lining togther. Sew Top Head Panel to top of Right and Left Sides. Sew back seam. Sew Chest to Right and Left Sides, with CO edge at Tail and BO edge at front of Head, leaving open spaces at each end for Tail and Beak. Stuff body firmly with stuffing through Wing slits. Insert CO edges of Wings into slits and sew in place.

Upper Beak: With RS facing, using dpns and D, pick up and knit 5 sts along upper edge of beak opening. Purl 1 row.

Decrease Row 1 (RS): Ssk, k1, k2tog—3 sts remain. Purl 1 row.

Decrease Row 2: S2kp2—1 st remains. Fasten off.

Lower Beak: Work as for Upper Beak, picking up sts along lower edge of beak opening. Sew Upper and Lower Beaks together.

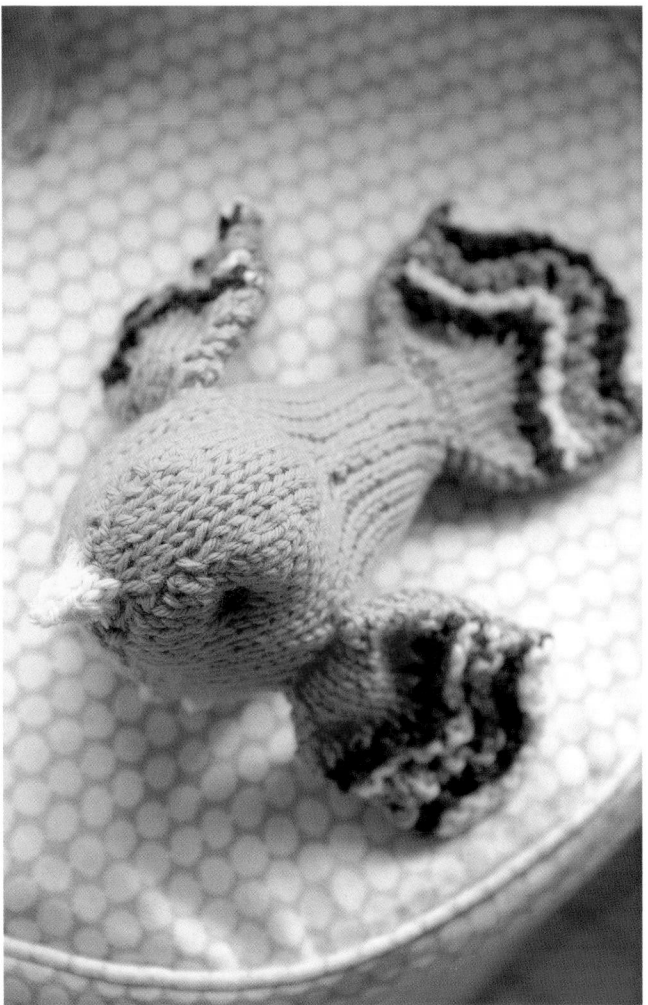

Eyes: With tapestry needle and C, insert needle into one side of Head and out the opposite side. Draw yarn through Head, leaving a 4" tail. Embroider one eye using satin st (see Special Techniques, page 156). Insert yarn through head to opposite side, just above 4" tail. Pull up yarn slightly, drawing Head together, knot end, leaving a 4" tail. Trim first tail short. Embroider second eye using satin st and working over short tail. Fasten off securely.

Feet: Using dpns and D, CO 2 sts. Work I-Cord (see Special Techniques, page 156) for 1½". Fasten off. Make a slip knot and place on dpn, then pick up and knit 1 st in first st of I-cord—2 sts. Work I-Cord for 1". Fasten off. Repeat for third toe, picking up 1 st in second st of first I-Cord. Sew Feet to Chest so that end of toes show when bird is sitting.

Havilland Blanket

The closer you look at this blanket, the more beautiful it becomes. A solid shade of yarn and a subtly variegated yarn are combined in an easy striped and textured stitch, with the printed shade creating a contrasting halo. When you look closely at both the pink and blue versions of this blanket, you see that both are sprinkled with many other hues.

FINISHED MEASUREMENTS
36" wide x 42½" long

YARN
Berroco Comfort DK (50% super fine nylon / 50% super fine acrylic; 50 grams / 178 yards):
Boys' Version: 5 skeins #2844 Twinkles (A); 2 skeins each #2747 Cadet (B), #2842 Puppies (C), and #2845 Fairies (D)
Girls' Version: 5 skeins #2843 Kittens (A); 2 skeins each #2723 Rosebud (B), #2840 Clouds (C), and #2842 Puppies (D)

NEEDLES
One pair straight needles size US 6 (4 mm)
One 29" (70 cm) long or longer circular (circ) needle size US 6 (4 mm)
Change needle size if necessary to obtain correct gauge.

GAUGE
22 sts and 32 rows = 4" (10 cm) in Navajo Basket Stitch

STITCH PATTERNS
NAVAJO BASKET STITCH (multiple of 4 sts + 3; 16-row repeat)
Row 1 (RS): Knit.
Row 2: Purl.
Row 3: K1, *slip 1 wyif, k1; repeat from * to end.
Row 4: Purl.

Row 5: K2, *slip 1 wyif, k1; repeat from * to last st, k1.
Row 6: Purl.
Rows 7 and 9: K1, *slip 1 wyib, k3; repeat from * to last 2 sts, slip 1 wyib, k1.
Rows 8 and 10: P1, *slip 1 wyif, p3; repeat from * to last 2 sts, slip 1 wyif, p1.
Rows 11-16: Repeat Rows 1-6.
Repeat Rows 1-16 for Navajo Basket st.

MOSS STITCH (even number of sts; 4-row repeat)
Row 1: *K1, p1; repeat from * to end.
Row 2: Knit the knit sts and purl the purl sts as they face you.
Row 3: Purl the knit sts and knit the purl sts as they face you.
Row 4: Repeat Row 2.
Repeat Rows 1-4 for Moss st.

STRIPE SEQUENCE
Working in Navajo Basket Stitch, *work 2 rows A, 2 rows B, 2 rows A, then 4 rows C; repeat from * for Stripe Sequence.

STRIPS 1 AND 2

Using straight needles and A, CO 63 sts. Begin Navajo Basket Stitch and Stripe Sequence; work even until piece measures 40" from the beginning, ending with a purl row. BO all sts.

STRIP 3

Using straight needles and A, CO 63 sts. Begin Navajo Basket Stitch and Stripe Sequence, beginning with Row 11 of Navajo Basket Stitch; work even until piece measures 40" from the beginning, ending with a purl row. BO all sts.

FINISHING

Strip 3 Borders: Using circ needle and D, pick up and knit 220 sts evenly along one side of Strip 3. Begin Moss st; work even for 4 rows. BO all sts in pattern. Repeat for opposite edge. Sew Strips 1 and 2 to each side of Strip 3.

Outside Borders: Using circ needle and D, pick up and knit 220 sts evenly along side edge of Strip 1. Begin Moss st; work even for 4 rows. BO all sts in pattern. Repeat for side edge of Strip 2.

Top and Bottom Borders: Using circ needle and D, pick up, and knit 204 sts evenly along top edge of Blanket, including Outside Borders. Begin Moss st; work even for 4 rows. BO all sts in pattern. Repeat for bottom edge.

Block lightly (see Special Techniques, page 156).

Limoges
Blanket

This round blanket pays homage to pale blue Limoges teacups from the Victorian era and the delicate doilies on which they were often laid. The arcs of cluster stitches swirl softly inward and converge at the center of this sweet blanket.

FINISHED MEASUREMENTS
38½" diameter

YARN
Berroco Vintage Chunky (50% acrylic / 40% wool / 10% nylon; 100 grams / 130 yards): 8 hanks #6112 Minty

CROCHET HOOKS
One crochet hook size US J/10 (6 mm)
Change hook size if necessary to obtain correct gauge.

GAUGE
12 sts and 14 rows = 4" (10 cm) in Single Crochet (sc)

ABBREVIATION
Puff Stitch (PS): Worked around the post of the tr in rnd below, [yo, insert hook and pull through a loop, elongating the loop to top of row] 4 times, then yo and pull yarn through 8 loops on hook, yo, pull yarn through last 2 loops on hook.

BLANKET
Ch 5, slip st in first ch to form a ring.
Rnd 1: Ch 3 (counts as 1 dc), work 12 dc in ring, join with a slip st in top of beginning ch-3—13 dc.
Rnd 2: Ch 3 (counts as 1 dc), work 1 dc in base of ch-3, 2 dc in each dc around, slip st in top of beginning ch-3—26 dc.
Rnd 3: Ch 3 (counts as 1 dc), 1 dc and 1 tr in the next dc [dc in next dc, 1 dc and 1 tr in next dc] 12 times, slip st in top of beginning ch-3—39 sts.
Rnd 4: Ch 3 (counts as 1 dc), 2 dc in next dc, [PS around next tr, dc in next dc, 2 dc in next dc] 12 times, PS around next tr, slip st in top of beginning ch-3—52 sts.
Rnd 5: Ch 3 (counts as 1 dc), 1 dc in next dc, 2 dc in next dc, [tr in next PS, dc in each dc to 1 dc before PS, 2 dc in next dc] 12 times, dc in next dc, tr in PS, slip st in top of beginning ch-3—65 sts.
Rnd 6: Ch 3 (counts as 1 dc), 2 dc in next dc, [dc in each dc to next tr, PS around next tr, dc in next dc, 2 dc in next dc] 12 times, dc in next 2 dc, PS around next tr, slip st in top of beginning ch-3—78 sts.
Repeat Rnds 5 and 6, increasing 13 sts each rnd, until piece measures 36" in diameter, ending with Rnd 6.

FINISHING
EDGING
Rnd 1: Ch 3 (counts as 1 dc), *tr in next st, dc in next st; repeat from * to end, slip st in top of beginning ch-3.
Rnd 2: Ch 1, *PS around next tr, sc in next dc; repeat from * to end, PS around last tr, slip st in top of ch 1. Fasten off.

Block lightly (see Special Techniques, page 156).

Dickie
Sweater

This fun retro sweater is inspired by children's fashion from the 1930s, when plaids and argyles peeked from beneath tweed jackets. The high-contrast color choice serves to heighten the nostalgic appeal, but you may prefer to choose more closely matched shades for a subtler statement.

SIZES
3 (6, 9, 12, 18, 24) months

FINISHED MEASUREMENTS
18½ (19½, 20½, 23, 24, 26½)" chest

YARN
Berroco Comfort (50% super fine nylon / 50% super fine acrylic; 100 grams / 210 yards): 2 (2, 2, 2, 2, 3) skeins #9716 Chambray (A); 1 skein #9703 Barley (B)

CROCHET HOOKS
Crochet hook size US J/10 (6 mm)
Change hook size if necessary to obtain correct gauge.

GAUGE
14 sts and 12 rows = 4" (10 cm) in Striped Pattern
14 sts and 11 rows = 4" (10 cm) in Sleeve Pattern

ABBREVIATIONS
FPdc: Yo, insert hook from front to back to front around post of next dc, yo and pull up a loop, [yo and pull through 2 loops on hook] twice.
BPdc: Yo, insert hook from back to front to back around post of next dc, yo and pull up a loop, [yo and pull through 2 loops on hook] twice.

STITCH PATTERNS
Note: All stitch patterns are reversible.
DOUBLE CROCHET RIB (even number of sts + 2 ch; 1-row repeat)
Row 1: Dc in third ch from hook and in each ch to end, turn.
Row 2: Ch 2 (does not count as a st), *FPdc in next dc, BPdc in next dc; repeat from * to end, turn.
Repeat Row 2 for Double Crochet Rib.

STRIPED PATTERN (multiple of 8 sts + 4; 2-row repeat)
Using B, ch appropriate number of sts.
Row 1: Dc in fourth ch from hook and in next 2 ch sts, *sc in next 4 ch sts, dc in next 4 ch sts; repeat from * to end, pull up a long loop in last st. Do not turn or cut yarn; remove hook from long loop and return to beginning of row just worked.
Row 2: Join A (or change to A on subsequent repeats) to third ch of beginning ch, ch 1, sc in first 4 sts, *dc in next 4 sc, sc in next 4 dc; repeat from * to end, working last pull-through of final st with loop of color B from Row 1, turn. Do not cut yarn.
Row 3: Using B, ch 3, skip first sc, dc in next 3 sc, *sc in next 4 dc, dc in next 4 sc; repeat from * to end, pull up a long loop in last st. Do not turn or cut yarn; remove hook from long loop and return to beginning of row just worked.
Repeat Rows 2 and 3 for Striped Pattern.

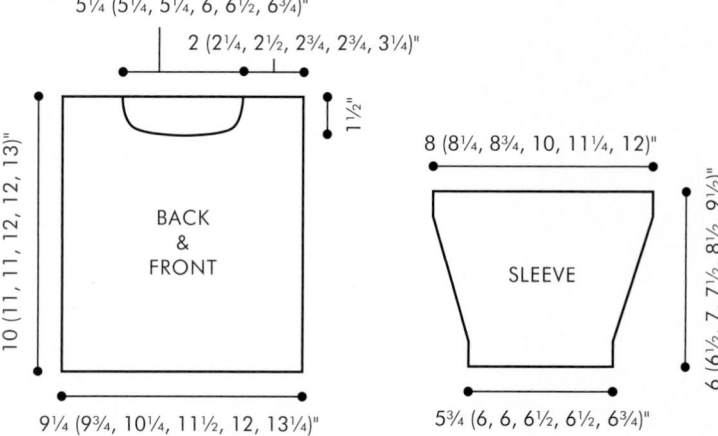

5¼ (5¼, 5¼, 6, 6½, 6¾)"

2 (2¼, 2½, 2¾, 2¾, 3¼)"

1½"

BACK & FRONT

10 (11, 11, 12, 12, 13)"

9¼ (9¾, 10¼, 11½, 12, 13¼)"

8 (8¼, 8¾, 10, 11¼, 12)"

SLEEVE

6 (6½, 7, 7½, 8½, 9½)"

5¾ (6, 6, 6½, 6½, 6¾)"

SLEEVE PATTERN (any number of sts; 2-row repeat)
Row 1: Ch 1, sc in each ch to end, turn.
Row 2: Ch 2, skip first sc, dc in each sc to end, turn.
Row 3: Ch 1, sc in each dc to end, turn.
Repeat Rows 2 and 3 for Sleeve Pattern.

BACK

With A, ch 34 (36, 38, 42, 44, 48). Begin Double Crochet Rib; work even for 3 rows, ending last pull-through of final dc with B—32 (34, 36, 40, 42, 46) sts.
Change to B and Striped Pattern as follows:

SIZES 3, 6, AND 9 MONTHS ONLY
Row 1: Ch 3 (counts as dc), skip first st, dc in next 1 (2, 3, -, -, -) sts, sc in next 4 sts, *dc in next 4 sts, sc in next 4 sts; repeat from * to end, ending with dc in last 2 (3, 4, -, -, -) sts, pull up a long loop in last st. Do not turn or cut yarn; remove hook from long loop and return to beginning of row just worked.
Row 2: Join A (or change to A on subsequent repeats) to third ch of beginning ch, ch 1, sc in first 2 (3, 4, -, -, -) sts, dc in next 4 sc, *sc in next 4 dc, dc in next 4 sc; repeat from * to end, ending with sc in last 2 (3, 4, -, -, -) dc, and working last pull-through of final st with loop of color B from Row 1, turn. Do not cut yarn.
Row 3: With B, ch 3, skip first sc, dc in next 1 (2, 3, -, -, -) sc, sc in next 4 dc, *dc in next 4 sc, sc in next 4 dc; repeat from *, ending with dc in last 2 (3, 4, -, -, -) sc. Pull up a long loop in last st. Do not turn or cut yarn.
Repeat Rows 2 and 3 for Striped Pattern.

SIZES 12, 18, AND 24 MONTHS ONLY
Row 1: Ch 1, sc in first - (-, -, 2, 3, 5) sts, dc in next 4 sts, *sc in next 4 sts, dc in next 4 sts; repeat from * across, ending with sc in last - (-, -, 2, 3, 5) sts, pull up a long loop in last st. Do not turn or cut yarn; remove hook from long loop and return to beginning of row just worked.
Row 2: Join A (or change to A on subsequent repeats) in first sc, ch 3, skip first sc, dc in next - (-, -, 1, 2, 4) sc, sc in next 4 dc, *dc in next 4 sc, sc in next 4 dc; repeat from *, to end, ending with dc in last - (-, -, 2, 3, 5) sc, and working last pull-through of final st with loop of color B from Row 1, turn. Do not cut yarn.
Row 3: With B, ch 1, sc in first - (-, -, 2, 3, 5) sts, dc in next 4 sc, *sc in next 4 dc, dc in next 4 sc; repeat from * to end, ending with sc in last - (-, -, 2, 3, 5) dc. Pull up a long loop in last st. Do not turn or cut yarn.
Repeat Rows 2 and 3 for Striped Pattern.

ALL SIZES
Work even until Back measures 10 (11, 11, 12, 12, 13)" from the beginning. Fasten off. Place markers 7 (8, 9, 10, 10, 11) sts in from each edge for shoulders.

FRONT

Work as for Back until piece is 5 rows shorter than Back.
Work 10 (11, 12, 13, 13, 14) sts, turn, leaving remaining sts unworked. Working first shoulder only, work even for 1 row. Decrease 1 st at neck edge every row 3 times—7 (8, 9, 10, 10, 11) sts remain. Fasten off.

Skipping 12 (12, 12, 14, 16, 18) sts to left of last st made in first shoulder, rejoin appropriate color in next st, work to end—10 (11, 12, 13, 13, 14) sts remain. Complete as for first shoulder.

SLEEVES

With A, ch 21 (22, 22, 24, 24, 25). Working even on 20 (21, 21, 23, 23, 24) sts, begin Sleeve Pattern; work even for 1".

Shape Sleeves: Increase 1 st each side this row, then every other row 1 (1, 1, 3, 4, 5) time(s), then every 4 rows 2 (2, 3, 2, 3, 3) times—28 (29, 31, 35, 39, 42) sts. Work even until piece measures 6 (6½, 7, 7½, 8½, 9½)" from the beginning, ending with a sc row. Fasten off.

FINISHING

Sew one shoulder seam.

Neckband: With RS facing, using A and beginning at neck edge, ch 2 (does not count as a st), work 44 (44, 44, 46, 48, 50) dc evenly spaced along neck edge, turn. Begin Double Crochet Rib; work even for 2 rows. Fasten off. Sew second shoulder seam. Sew side edges of Neckband together.

Place markers 4 (4¼, 4½, 5, 5½, 6)" down from shoulders on Front and Back. Sew Sleeves between markers. Sew side and Sleeve seams.

Sunday Best
Dress

We used a combination of solid and subtly variegated yarns to create this new take on an old-fashioned "Sunday best" dress. Single crochet worked through the back loop gives the skirt and sleeves the illusion of miniature pleats, while the wave stitch on the yoke is highlighted by the color changes.

SIZES
3 (6, 9, 12, 18, 24) months

FINISHED MEASUREMENTS
18 (19½, 20, 22, 24½, 26)" chest

YARN
Berroco Comfort DK (50% super fine nylon / 50% super fine acrylic; 50 grams / 178 yards): 3 (3, 3, 3, 4, 4) skeins #2840 Clouds (MC); 1 skein each #2704 Peach (A), #2811 Multi Baby (B), and #2709 Menthe (C)

CROCHET HOOKS
One crochet hook size US F/5 (3.75 mm)
Change hook size if necessary to obtain correct gauge.

GAUGE
22 sts and 26 rows = 4" (10 cm) in Single Crochet-tbl (sc-tbl)

STITCH PATTERNS
WAVY SHELL STITCH (multiple of 14 sts + 1 + 2 ch; 4-row repeat)
Set-Up Row (RS): Dc in third ch from hook, 2 dc in same ch, *skip next 3 chs, sc in next 7 chs, skip next 3 chs, 7 dc in next ch; repeat from *, end last repeat 4 dc in last ch, turn.
Row 1: Ch 1, sc in each st to end, sc in top of beginning ch, turn.
Row 2: Ch 1, sc in first 4 sc, *skip next 3 sc, 7 dc in next sc, skip next 3 sc, sc in next 7 sc; repeat from *, end last repeat sc in last 4 sc, turn.
Row 3: Ch 1, sc in each st to end, turn.
Row 4: Ch 3, 3 dc in first sc, *skip next 3 sc, sc in next 7 sc, skip next 3 sc, 7 dc in next sc; repeat from *, end last repeat 4 dc in last sc, turn.
Repeat Rows 1-4 for Wavy Shell Stitch.

STRIPE SEQUENCE
Working in Wavy Shell Stitch, *work one row each in A, B, then C; repeat from * for Stripe Sequence.

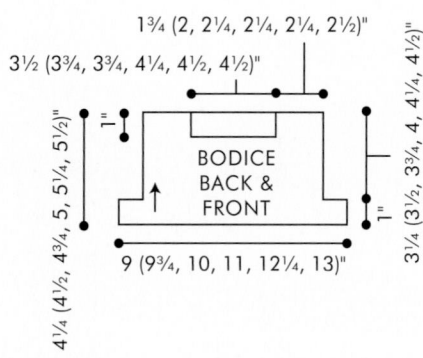

1¾ (2, 2¼, 2¼, 2¼, 2½)"

3½ (3¾, 3¾, 4¼, 4½, 4½)"

1"

BODICE
BACK &
FRONT

4¼ (4½, 4¾, 5, 5¼, 5½)"

3¼ (3½, 3¾, 4, 4¼, 4½)"

1"

9 (9¾, 10, 11, 12¼, 13)"

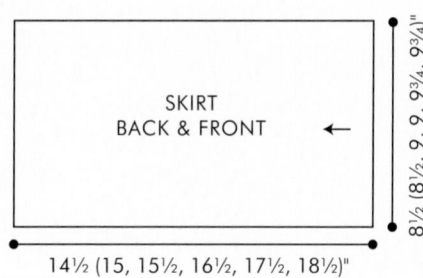

SKIRT
BACK & FRONT

8½ (8½, 9, 9, 9¾, 9¾)"

14½ (15, 15½, 16½, 17½, 18½)"

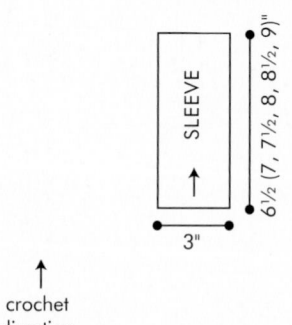

SLEEVE

6½ (7, 7½, 8, 8½, 9)"

3"

↑
crochet
direction

SKIRT

Using MC, ch 48 (48, 50, 50, 54, 54). Begin sc-tbl; work even until piece measures 14½ (15, 15½, 16½, 17½, 18½)" from the beginning—47 (47, 49, 49, 53, 53) sc. Fasten off.

BACK BODICE

Turn Skirt and using MC, work 49 (53, 55, 61, 67, 71) sc across one long edge. *Note: This will gather in Skirt.*
Next Row (RS): Using A, ch 1, work sc in next 3 (5, 6, 2, 5, 7) sc, work Stripe Sequence and Wavy Shell Stitch, beginning with Row 2, over next 43 (43, 43, 57, 57, 57) sts, end sc in last 3 (5, 6, 2, 5, 7) sc. Work even for 3 rows.

SHAPE ARMHOLES

Next Row (RS): Slip st into first 5 (5, 5, 7, 9, 9) sts, work to last 5 (5, 5, 7, 9, 9) sts, turn—39 (43, 45, 47, 49, 53) sts remain. Work even until armhole measures 3¼ (3½, 3¾, 4, 4¼, 4½)", ending with a WS row. Fasten off.

FRONT BODICE

Work as for Back Bodice until armholes measure 2¼ (2½, 2¾, 3, 3¼, 3½)", ending with a WS row—39 (43, 45, 47, 49, 53) sts remain.

SHAPE NECK

Next Row (RS): Work 10 (11, 12, 12, 12, 14) sts, skip center 19 (21, 21, 23, 25, 25) sts, join a second ball of yarn, and work to end. Working both sides at the same time, work even until armhole measures same as for Back Bodice, ending with a WS row. Fasten off.

SLEEVES

Using MC, ch 18. Begin sc-tbl; work even until piece measures 6½ (7, 7½, 8, 8½, 9)" from the beginning—17 sc. Fasten off.

FINISHING

Sew shoulder seams. Set in Sleeves. Sew side, Sleeve, and Bodice seams.

Neckband: Using MC, work 1 rnd sc around neck shaping.

Citron Blanket

A hooded blanket is a useful and cozy way to keep a baby or toddler warm after a bath. And when the child is a little older, the same blanket makes a perfect costume for a game of superhero dress-up.

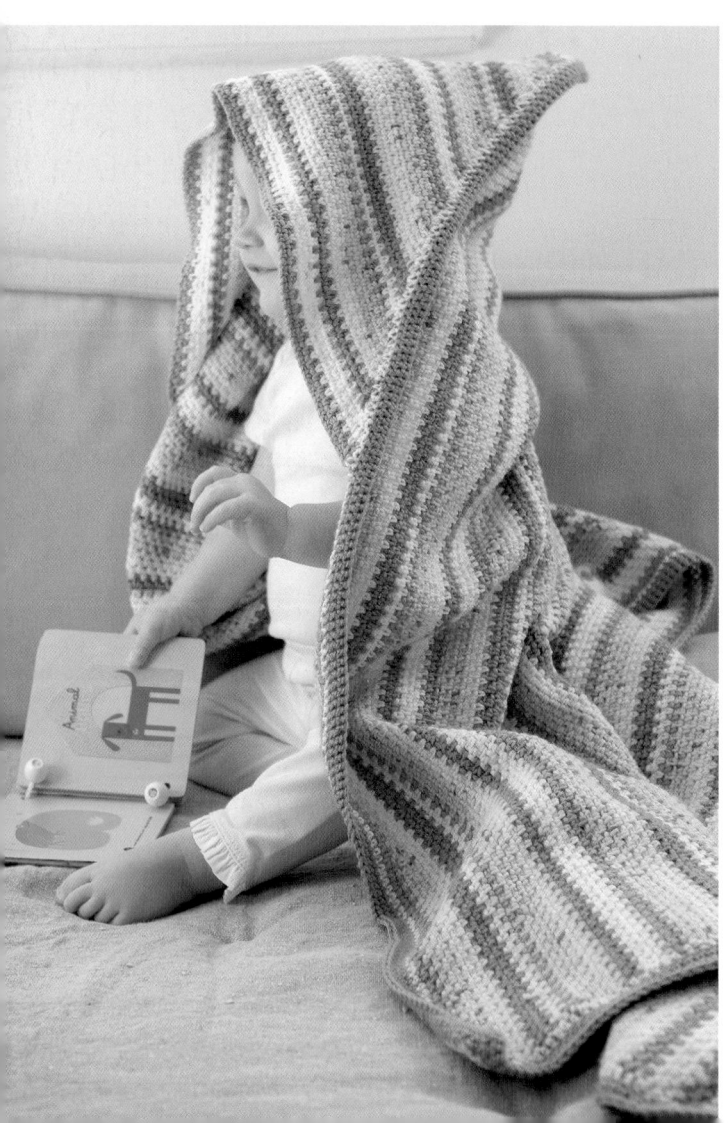

FINISHED MEASUREMENTS
37¼" wide x 37½" long

YARN
Berroco Comfort DK (50% super fine nylon / 50% super fine acrylic; 50 grams / 178 yards):
Boys' Version: 4 skeins each #2842 Puppies (A), #2721 Sprig (B), and #2845 Fairies (C); 2 skeins each #2761 Lovage (D), #2704 Peach (E), and #2733 Turquoise (F)
Girls' Version: 4 skeins each #2843 Kittens (A), #2721 Sprig (B), and #2845 Fairies (C); 2 skeins each #2723 Rosebud (D), #2719 Sunshine (E), and #2704 Peach (F)

CROCHET HOOKS
One crochet hook size US G/6 (4 mm)
Change hook size if necessary to obtain correct gauge.

GAUGE
24 sts and 22 rows = 4" (10 cm) in Seed stitch

STITCH PATTERNS
SEED STITCH (odd number of sts + 1 ch; 2-row repeat)
Set-Up Row: Sc in second ch from hook, *ch 1, skip next ch, sc in next ch; repeat from * to end, turn.
Row 1: Ch 2 (counts as 1 sc and ch-1 sp), *sc in ch-1 sp, skip next sc, ch 1; repeat from * to end, sc in last ch, turn.
Row 2: Ch 1, sc in first ch-1 sp, *ch 1, skip next sc, sc in next ch-1 sp; repeat from * to end, turn.
Repeat Rows 1 and 2 for Seed St.

STRIPE SEQUENCE

Work *2 rows D, 4 rows A, 2 rows B, 3 rows E, 1 row F, then 4 rows C; repeat from * for Stripe Sequence.

BLANKET

Using D, ch 216. Begin Seed st; work even for 1 row—215 sts remain.

Next Row: Continuing in Seed st, begin Stripe Sequence; work even until piece measures 36" from the beginning. Fasten off.

CORNER POCKET/HOOD

Using D, ch 126 sts. Begin Seed st; work even for 1 row—125 sts remain.

SHAPE CORNER POCKET/HOOD

Next Row: Continuing in Seed st, begin Stripe Sequence, decrease 1 st each side every row 61 times—3 sts remain. Fasten off. Sew Corner Pocket/Hood to one corner of Blanket.

FINISHING

Using A, work 1 rnd sc around entire Blanket, working 3 sc in each corner. Change to C; work 3 rnds sc around Blanket, working 3 sc in each corner.

Block lightly (see Special Techniques, page 156).

Tuxedo
Romper

This all-in-one romper was inspired by a pleated and ruffled tuxedo shirt. An easy texture stitch lends the illusion of pleats, and a knitted ruffle cascades down the front and around the neckline for added dimension and interest. Snaps along the front and on the legs allow for quick changes.

SIZES
3 (6, 9, 12) months

FINISHED MEASUREMENTS
19 (20, 22, 24½)" chest

YARN
Berroco Vintage (50% acrylic / 40% wool / 10% nylon; 100 grams / 217 yards): 2 hanks #5120 Gingham

NEEDLES
One pair straight needles size US 8 (5 mm)
One pair straight needles size US 7 (4.5 mm)
Change needle size if necessary to obtain correct gauge

NOTIONS
8 medium snaps

GAUGE
18 sts and 24 rows = 4" (10 cm) in Stockinette stitch (St st), using larger needles

ABBREVIATION
M2 (Make 2): With the tip of the left-hand needle inserted from front to back, lift the strand between the two needles onto the left-hand needle; knit the strand through the front loop then the back loop to increase 2 sts.

STITCH PATTERN
RIB PATTERN (odd number of sts; 2-row repeat)
Row 1 (RS): K1, *p1, k1; repeat from * to end.
Row 2: Purl.
Repeat Rows 1 and 2 for Rib Pattern.

LEFT SIDE
Using larger needles, CO 61 (63, 67, 73) sts. Begin Rib Pattern; work even for 4 rows.
Next Row (RS): Change to St st; work even for 1", ending with a WS row.

SHAPE CUFF
Next Row (RS): BO 4 sts at beginning of next 2 rows, then decrease 1 st each side every other row 5 times, as follows: K2tog, work to last 2 sts, ssk—43 (45, 49, 55) sts remain. Knit 1 row.

SHORT-ROW SHAPING
Row 1 (RS): Continuing in St st, work 5 sts, turn, work to end.
Row 2: Work 10 sts, turn, work to end.
Row 3: Work 14 sts, turn, work to end. Continuing in St st, work even until piece measures 5½" from the beginning, ending with a RS row. Place marker at end of this row to mark end of lower front. Work even until piece measures 11½" from the beginning, ending with a WS row.
Next Row (RS): Work to last 7 sts, work in Rib Pattern to end. Work even for 5 rows.

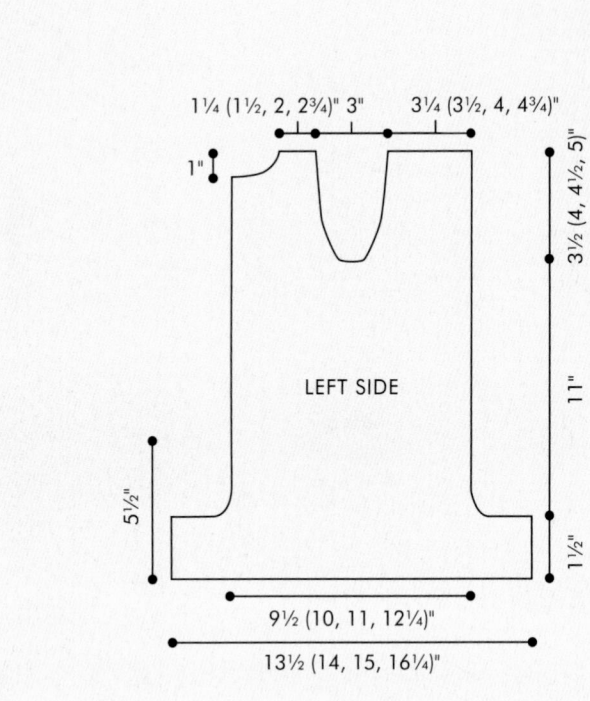

1¼ (1½, 2, 2¾)" 3"   3¼ (3½, 4, 4¾)"

1"

3½ (4, 4½, 5)"

LEFT SIDE

11"

5½"

1½"

9½ (10, 11, 12¼)"

13½ (14, 15, 16¼)"

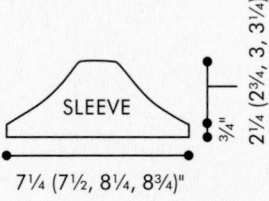

SLEEVE

2¼ (2¾, 3, 3¼)"

¾"

7¼ (7½, 8¼, 8¾)"

SHAPE ARMHOLE

Next Row (RS): Work 19 (20, 22, 25) sts, join a second ball of yarn and BO center 5 sts, work to end. Working both sides at the same time, decrease 1 st at each armhole edge every other row 4 times—15 (16, 18, 21) sts remain each side. Work even until armhole measures 2½ (3, 3½, 4)", ending with a RS row.

SHAPE NECK

Next Row (WS): BO 5 sts at neck edge once, then decrease 1 st at neck edge every row 4 times, as follows: On RS rows, work to last 4 sts, k2tog, k2; on WS rows, p2, p2tog, purl to end.

Next Row (RS): BO remaining 6 (7, 9, 12) sts for Front shoulder and 15 (16, 18, 21) sts for Back shoulder and neck.

RIGHT SIDE

Work as for Left Side, reversing all shaping and pattern placement, and beginning short-row shaping on a WS row.

SLEEVES

Using larger needles, CO 33 (35, 37, 39) sts. Begin Rib Pattern; work even for 4 rows.

Shape Cap (RS): BO 3 sts at beginning of next 2 rows, decrease 1 st each side every other row 3 (4, 5, 6) times, then every row 6 times, as follows: On RS rows, k2tog, work to last 2 sts, ssk; on WS rows, p2tog, work to last 2 sts, p2tog-tbl. BO remaining 9 sts.

FINISHING

Sew Left Side to Right Side from center Back neck to beginning of crotch shaping. Sew Fronts from markers to beginning of crotch shaping. Sew shoulder seams. Sew in Sleeves. Sew Sleeve seams.

Crotch Edging: With RS facing, using smaller needles, pick up and knit 19 sts along Back crotch. Begin Rib Pattern; work even for 3 rows. BO all sts in pattern. Repeat for Front crotch.

Left Front Band: With RS facing, using smaller needles, pick up and knit 36 (40, 40, 44) sts along Left Front edge. Knit 2 rows. BO all sts knitwise.

Right Front Ruffle Band: With RS facing, using smaller needles, pick up and knit 44 (48, 48, 52) sts along Right Front edge. Purl 1 row.
Next Row (RS): *[K1, M1] 3 times, k1, M2; repeat from * to end—99 (108, 108, 117) sts. Purl 1 row. BO all sts knitwise.

Neckband: With RS facing, using smaller needles, pick up and knit 14 (15, 16, 19) sts along Right Front neck edge, 14 (18, 20, 20) sts across Back, and 14 (15, 16, 19) sts along Left Front neck edge—42 (48, 52, 58) sts. Purl 1 row.
Eyelet Row (RS): *K1, yo, k1; repeat from * to end—63 (72, 78, 87) sts. Purl 1 row. BO all sts knitwise.

Sew 3 snaps to crotch opening. Sew snaps to Front Bands, the first ½" below neck edge, the second ½" above bottom edge of Front Bands, and the remaining 3 snaps evenly spaced between.

Post & Beam
Blanket

Referencing midcentury modern post-and-beam architecture, our blanket has both strong horizontal and vertical elements and a sense of airiness. The unusual color palette reinforces the feeling of modernity while still feeling sweet enough for a baby.

FINISHED MEASUREMENTS
38" wide x 48" long

YARN
Berroco Comfort (50% super fine nylon / 50% super fine acrylic; 100 grams / 210 yards): 5 skeins #9703 Barley (A); 3 skeins each #9715 Lavender Frost (C) and #9713 Dusk (D); 1 skein #9740 Seedling (B)

CROCHET HOOKS
One crochet hook size US H/8 (5 mm)
Change hook size if necessary to obtain correct gauge.

GAUGE
14 sts and 17 rows = 4" (10 cm) in Single Crochet (sc)

BLANKET
Using A, ch 131. Begin sc; work even until piece measures 3½" from the beginning—130 sc.
Next Row: Change to B; work even for 1".
**Next Row: Change to D; sc in first 26 sc; *change to C; sc in next 26 sc; change to D; sc in next 26 sc; repeat from * to end. Work even for 3 rows.
Next Row: Change to A; sc in first 26 sc; *change to C; sc in next 26 sc; change to A; sc in next 26 sc; repeat from * to end. Work even for 1 row. Repeat from ** 9 times.
Next Row: Change to D; sc in first 26 sc; *change to C; sc in next 26 sc; change to D; sc in next 26 sc; repeat from * to end. Work even for 3 rows.*** Change to A; work even for 3½". Change to B; work even for 1". Change to A; work even for 3½". Repeat from ** to *** once more. Change to B; work even for 1". Change to A; work even for 3½". Fasten off.

FINISHING
Using A; work 2 rnds of sc evenly around entire Blanket, working 3 sc in each corner.

Block lightly (see Special Techniques, page 156).

Hike Hat

We interpreted this "helmet" pattern two ways to create distinctly different results. The version at right is color-blocked in bold shades and stays on with double buttons under the chin. The striped version, shown below, ties under the chin and is worked in two shades of plum, highlighting the arcs of the interesting construction.

FINISHED MEASUREMENTS
21½" circumference

YARN
Berroco Vintage Chunky (50% acrylic / 40% wool / 10% nylon; 100 grams / 130 yards):
Color-Blocked Hat: 1 hank each #6194 Breezeway (MC) and #6121 Sunny (A)
Striped Hat: 1 hank each #6180 Dried Plum (MC) and #6183 Lilacs (A)

NEEDLES
One pair straight needles size US 10 (6 mm)
One 16" (40 cm) long circular (circ) needle size US 10 (6 mm)
One pair double-pointed needles (dpn) size US 10 (6 mm), for Striped Hat Only
Change needle size if necessary to obtain correct gauge.

NOTIONS
Stitch marker; stitch holder; two ⅞" buttons

GAUGE
14 sts and 32 rows = 4" (10 cm) in Garter stitch (knit every row)

STITCH PATTERN (Striped hat only)
STRIPE SEQUENCE
Working in Garter st (knit every row), * work 2 rows in MC, then 2 rows in A; repeat from * for Stripe Sequence.

NOTE

Instructions for the color-blocked Hat are given first, followed by instructions for the striped Hat in parentheses. Where only one set of instructions is given, it applies to both versions.

CENTER PANEL

Using straight needles and A (MC), CO 13 sts.

Begin Garter st (Stripe Sequence); work even for 22 rows.
Decrease Row (RS): Decrease 1 st each side this row, then every 8 rows once, as follows: K1, k2tog, knit to last 3 sts, ssk, k1—9 sts remain. Knit 11 rows.
Increase Row (RS): Increase 1 st each side this row, then every 8 rows 3 times, as follows: K1, M1, knit to last st, M1, k1—17 sts. Knit 5 rows. Cut yarn and transfer sts to st holder.

SIDE PANELS

With RS facing, using circ needle and MC, pick up and knit 37 sts along one side edge of Center Panel. Begin Garter st (Stripe Sequence); work even for 5 rows.
Decrease Row 1 (RS): *K2, k2tog; repeat from * to last st, k1—28 sts remain. Knit 5 rows.
Decrease Row 2: *K1, k2tog; repeat from * to last st, k1—19 sts remain. Knit 5 rows.
Decrease Row 3: *K2tog; repeat from * to last st, k1—10 sts remain. Knit 3 rows.
Decrease Row 4: *K2tog; repeat from * to end—5 sts remain. Cut yarn, leaving an 8" tail; thread through remaining sts, pull tight, and fasten off. Repeat for opposite side.

BAND

With RS facing, using circ needle and MC, and beginning at right-hand edge of Side Panel adjacent to sts on holder for Center Panel, pick up and knit 75 sts around entire piece, including sts on holder for Center Panel. Join for working in the rnd; pm for beginning of rnd. Begin Garter st (purl 1 rnd, knit 1 rnd); work even for 4 rnds.
Next Rnd: P54, BO next 25 sts, removing beginning-of-rnd marker when you come to it—50 sts remain.

SHAPE BAND

Decrease Row (RS): Change to working back and forth. Continuing in Garter st, decrease 1 st each side this row, then every other row once, as follows: K2, k2tog, knit to last 4 sts, ssk, k2—46 sts rem.

EARFLAPS

Next Row (WS): K17, join a second ball of yarn, BO next 12 sts knitwise, knit to end—17 sts remain each side for Earflaps.

SHAPE EARFLAPS

Decrease Row: Working both sides at the same time, decrease 1 st each side of each Earflap this row, every other row once, every 8 rows once, then every other row 3 (4) times, as follows: K2, k2tog, knit to last 4 sts, ssk, k2—5 (3) sts remain each side for Earflaps.

COLOR-BLOCKED HAT ONLY

Knit 1 row. Transfer left Earflap sts to st holder.

RIGHT STRAP

Working on Right Strap sts only, work even for 3". BO all sts.

LEFT STRAP

With RS facing, rejoin yarn to left Earflap sts. Work as for Right Strap, working buttonholes when piece measures 1¼" and 2½" from beginning of Strap, as follows: (RS) K2, yo, ssk, k1.

FINISHING

Sew buttons to Right Strap, opposite buttonholes.

STRIPED HAT ONLY

TIES

Working on one Earflap at a time, change to dpns; work I-cord (see Special Techniques, page 156) for 7". BO all sts. Repeat for other Earflap.

Camellia
Blanket

This blanket is made in five pieces: The center square is flanked by four long rectangles, each with a simple diagonal swath of blossoms. The fascinating, highly dimensional camellia blossoms are crocheted into the blanket as you go.

FINISHED MEASUREMENTS
36" wide x 36" long

YARN
Berroco Comfort (50% super fine nylon / 50% super fine acrylic; 100 grams / 210 yards): 7 skeins #9715 Lavender Frost

CROCHET HOOKS
One crochet hook size US H/8 (5 mm)
Change hook size if necessary to obtain correct gauge.

GAUGE
14 sts and 9 rows = 4" (10 cm) in Double Crochet (dc)

SPECIAL TERM
Rosette: Dc in next dc, work 6 dc along post of dc just worked, turn, then work 6 dc along post of previous dc, continue to work in next st in current row as directed.

RECTANGLES (make 4)
Ch 45. Begin dc; dc in fourth ch from hook and in each ch to end, turn—43 sts remain. (Beginning ch 3 counts as 1 dc.)
Next Row (RS): Ch 3 (counts as 1 dc), dc in next dc, work rosette, dc to end, turn. Work even for 1 row, turn.
Next Row: Ch 3, dc in next 3 dc, work rosette, dc to end, turn. Work even for 1 row, turn.
Next Row: Ch 3, dc in next 5 dc, work rosette, dc to end, turn. Work even for 1 row, turn.
*Work 1 more dc before next rosette, work rosette, dc to end, turn. Work even for 1 row, turn. Ch 3, work 2 more dc before next rosette, work rosette, dc to end, turn. Work even for 1 row; repeat from * 10 times.
Next Row: Ch 3, work 2 more dc before next rosette, work rosette, dc to end, turn. Work even for 1 row. Fasten off.

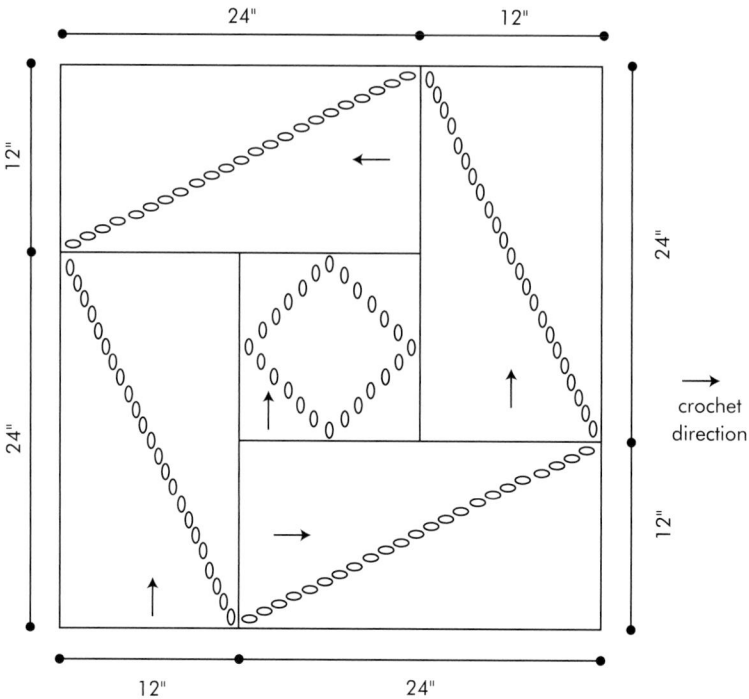

CENTER SQUARE

Ch 45. Begin dc; dc in fourth ch from hook and in each ch to end, turn—43 sts remain. (Beginning ch 3 counts as 1 dc.)
Next Row (RS): Ch 3 (counts as 1 dc), dc in next 20 dc, work rosette, dc to end, turn. Work even for 1 row, turn.
Next Row: Ch 3, dc in next 17 dc, work rosette, dc in next 5 dc, work rosette, dc to end, turn. Work even for 1 row.
Next Row: Ch 3, dc in next 13 dc, work rosette, dc in next 13 dc, work rosette, dc to end, turn. Work even for 1 row.
Next Row: Ch 3, dc in next 9 dc, work rosette, dc in next 21 dc, work rosette, dc to end, turn. Work even for 1 row.
Next Row: Ch 3, dc in next 6 dc, work rosette, dc in next 27 dc, work rosette, dc to end, turn. Work even for 1 row.
Next Row: Ch 3, dc in next 3 dc, work rosette, dc in next 33 dc, work rosette, dc to end, turn. Work even for 1 row.
Next Row: Ch 3, dc in next 1 dc, work rosette, dc in next 37 dc, work rosette, dc to end, turn. Work even for 1 row.
Next Row: Ch 3, dc in next 3 dc, work rosette, dc in next 33 dc, work rosette, dc to end, turn. Work even for 1 row.

Next Row: Ch 3, dc in next 6 dc, work rosette, dc in next 27 dc, work rosette, dc to end, turn. Work even for 1 row.
Next Row: Ch 3, dc in next 9 dc, work rosette, dc in next 21 dc, work rosette, dc to end, turn. Work even for 1 row.
Next Row: Ch 3, dc in next 13 dc, work rosette, dc in next 13 dc, work rosette, dc to end, turn. Work even for 1 row.
Next Row: Ch 3, dc in next 17 dc, work rosette, dc in next 5 dc, work rosette, dc to end, turn. Work even for 1 row.
Next Row: Ch 3, dc in next 20 dc, work rosette, dc to end, turn. Work even for 1 row. Fasten off.

FINISHING

Sew pieces together following Assembly Diagram.

Block lightly (see Special Techniques, page 156).

"Aran" Blanket

While this blanket's stitchwork looks like Aran knitting,
it's actually crochet. The earthy color and decorative design
keep it well rooted in Irish tradition.

FINISHED MEASUREMENTS
35" wide x 47½" long

YARN
Berroco Vintage DK (50% acrylic / 40% wool / 10% nylon; 100
grams / 288 yards): 9 hanks #2105 Oats

CROCHET HOOKS
Crochet hook size US G/6 (4 mm)
Change hook size if necessary to obtain correct gauge.

GAUGE
20 sts and 12 rows = 4" (10 cm) in Pattern Stitch

ABBREVIATIONS
FPdc: Yo, insert hook from front to back to front around post of
next dc, yo and pull up a loop, [yo and pull through 2 loops on
hook] twice.
BPdc: Yo, insert hook from back to front to back around post
of next dc, yo and pull up a loop, [yo and pull through 2 loops
on hook] twice.

STITCH PATTERN

PATTERN STITCH (multiple of 14 sts + 15 + 3 ch; 12-row repeat)

Row 1 (RS): Dc in fourth ch from hook and in each ch to end, turn.

Row 2: Ch 3 (counts as dc here and throughout), *BPdc in next 2 dc, dc in next 10 dc, BPdc in next 2 dc; repeat from * to end, dc in top of turning ch, turn.

Row 3: Ch 3, FPdc in next 2 BPdc, *dc in next 10 dc**, skip next 2 BPdc, FPdc in next 2 FPdc, working in front of 2 FPdc just worked, FPdc in 2 skipped BPdc; repeat from * to end, ending last repeat at **, FPdc in next 2 BPdc, dc in top of turning ch, turn.

Row 4: Ch 3, skip next 2 FPdc, *dc in next dc, working in the back of dc just worked, BPdc in 2 skipped FPdc, dc in next 8 dc, skip next dc, BPdc in next 2 FPdc, working in front of 2 BPdc just worked, dc in skipped dc; repeat from * to end, dc in top of turning ch, turn.

Row 5: Ch 3, *dc in next dc, skip next 2 BPdc, dc in next dc, working in front of dc just worked, FPdc in 2 skipped BPdc, dc in next 6 dc, skip next dc, FPdc in next 2 BPdc, working in back of 2 FPdc just worked, dc in skipped dc, dc in next dc; repeat from * to end, dc in top of turning ch, turn.

Row 6: Ch 3, *dc in next 2 dc, skip next 2 FPdc, dc in next dc, working in back of dc just worked, BPdc in 2 skipped FPdc, dc in next 4 dc, skip next dc, BPdc in next 2 FPdc, working in front of BPdc just worked, dc in skipped dc, dc in next 2 dc; repeat from * to end, dc in top of turning ch, turn.

Row 7: Ch 3, *dc in next 3 dc, skip next 2 BPdc, dc in next dc, working in front of dc just worked, FPdc in 2 skipped BPdc, dc in next 2 dc, skip next dc, FPdc in next 2 BPdc, working in back of 2 FPdc just worked, dc in skipped dc, dc in next 3 dc; repeat from * to end, dc in top of turning ch, turn.

Row 8: Ch 3, *dc in next 4 dc, skip next 2 FPdc, dc in next dc, working in back of dc just worked, BPdc in 2 skipped FPdc, skip next dc, BPdc in next 2 FPdc, working in front of 2 BPdc just worked, dc in skipped dc, dc in next 4 dc; repeat from * to end, dc in top of turning ch, turn.

Row 9: Ch 3, *dc in next 5 dc, skip next 2 BPdc, FPdc in next 2 BPdc, working in front of 2 FPdc just worked, FPdc in 2 skipped BPdc, dc in next 5 dc; repeat from * to end, dc in top of turning ch, turn.

Row 10: Ch 3, *dc in next 4 dc, skip next dc, BPdc in next 2 FPdc, working in front of 2 BPdc just worked, dc in skipped dc, skip next 2 dc, dc in next dc, working in back of dc just worked, BPdc in 2 skipped FPdc, dc in next 4 dc; repeat from * to end, dc in top of turning ch, turn.

Row 11: Ch 3, *dc in next 3 dc, skip next dc, FPdc in next 2 BPdc, working in back of 2 FPdc just worked, dc in skipped dc, dc in next 2 dc, skip next 2 dc, dc in next dc, working in

front of dc just worked, FPdc in 2 skipped BPdc, dc in next 3 dc; repeat from * to end, dc in top of turning ch, turn.

Row 12: Ch 3, *dc in 2 dc, skip next dc, BPdc in next 2 FPdc, working in front of 2 BPdc just worked, dc in skipped dc, dc in next 4 dc, skip next 2 FPdc, dc in next dc, working in back of dc just worked, BPdc in 2 skipped FPdc, dc in next 2 dc; repeat from * to end, dc in top of turning ch. Turn.

Row 13: Ch 3, *dc in next dc, skip next dc, FPdc in next 2 BPdc, working in back of 2 FPdc just worked, dc in skipped dc, dc in next 6 dc, skip next 2 BPdc, dc in next dc, working in front of dc just worked, FPdc in 2 skipped BPdc, dc in next dc; repeat from * to end, dc in top of turning ch, turn.

Row 14: Ch 3, *skip next dc, BPdc in next 2 FPdc, working in front of 2 BPdc just worked, dc in skipped dc, dc in next 8 dc, skip next 2 FPdc, dc in next dc, working in back of dc just worked, BPdc in 2 skipped FPdc; repeat from * to end, dc in top of turning ch, turn.

Repeat Rows 3-14 for Pattern Stitch.

BLANKET

Ch 144. Work Row 1 of Pattern Stitch—142 dc, turn. Work even until piece measures approximately 41" from the beginning, ending with Row 3 of Pattern Stitch. Work Row 2 of Pattern Stitch. Finish off.

FINISHING

BORDER

Rnd 1: With RS facing, join yarn in one corner of Blanket, ch 3, 2 dc in same st, *work 123 dc evenly spaced across short edge to next corner, 3 dc in next corner st, work 163 dc evenly spaced across long edge to next corner**, 3 dc in next corner st; repeat from * to ** once—583 dc, plus ch-3 at beginning of rnd. Join with a slip st in top of beginning ch-3. *Note: Be sure to work an odd number of dc on each edge between corners. Mark center dc of each corner.*

Rnd 2: Ch 3 (counts as BPdc), **FPdc in marked corner st, 2 BPdc in next dc, FPdc in next dc, *BPdc in next dc, FPdc in next dc; repeat from * to 1 st before next marked dc, 2 BPdc in next dc; repeat from ** around entire edge of Blanket, ending last repeat with BPdc in same space as beginning ch-3—592 post sts. Join with a slip st in top of beginning ch-3.

Rnd 3: Ch 3 (counts as BPdc), **FPdc in marked corner st, (BPdc, FPdc) in next dc, *BPdc in next dc, FPdc in next dc; repeat from * to 1 st before next marked dc, (FPdc, BPdc) in next dc; repeat from ** around entire edge of Blanket, ending last repeat with FPdc in same space as beginning ch-3—600 post sts. Join with a slip st in top of beginning ch-3.

Rnds 4-10: Repeat Rnds 2 and 3 three times, then repeat Rnd 2 once—648 post sts. Fasten off at end of last rnd.

Block lightly (see Special Techniques, page 156).

Plié
Cardigan

For this wrap cardigan, we used crochet stitches reminiscent of knitted cables and combined them with kimono styling. The body of the cardigan is pliable and soft, working up very quickly in double crochet. The fancy cable pattern requires a bit of concentration, so it's worked on a straight band and sewn on. Crossover styling and cuffed sleeves ensure that this cardigan will fit for a long time.

SIZES
3 (6, 9, 12, 18, 24) months

FINISHED MEASUREMENTS
17½ (19, 20, 22½, 24½, 25½)" chest

YARN
Berroco Vintage DK (50% acrylic / 40% wool / 10% nylon; 100 grams / 288 yards): 2 (2, 2, 3, 3, 3) hanks #2101 Mochi

CROCHET HOOKS
One crochet hook size US I/9 (5.5 mm)
Change hook size if necessary to obtain correct gauge.

GAUGE
14 sts and 13 rows = 4" (10 cm) in Extended Single Crochet (EXsc)

ABBREVIATIONS
FPdc: Yo, insert hook from front to back to front around post of indicated st, yo and pull up a loop, [yo and pull through 2 loops on hook] twice. Skip sc behind FPdc.
FPtr tr: Yo 4 times, insert hook from front to back to front around post of indicated st, yo and pull up a loop, [yo and pull through 2 loops on hook] 5 times. Skip sc behind FPtr tr.
EXsc: Insert hook in st, yo and pull loop through st, yo, pull through 1 loop on hook, yo, pull through 2 loops on hook.
EXsc2tog: [Insert hook in next st, yo and pull loop through st, yo, pull through 1 loop on hook] twice, yo, pull through 3 loops on hook.
EXsc3tog: [Insert hook in next st, yo and pull loop through st, yo, pull through 1 loop on hook] 3 times, yo, pull through 4 loops on hook.

STITCH PATTERNS
EXTENDED SINGLE CROCHET (EXsc) (any number of sts + 2 ch; 1-row repeat)
Note: Pattern is reversible.
Row 1: EXsc in third ch from hook and in each ch across, turn.
Row 2: Ch 2 (counts as 1 EXsc), skip first EXsc, 1 EXsc in each st across, ending 1 EXsc in top of beginning ch-2, turn.
Repeat Row 2 for Extended Single Crochet.

COLLAR PATTERN (panel of 15 sts; 12-row repeat)
Note: It is important to skip the next sc directly behind all FPdcs and FPtr trs.
Row 1 (RS): Sc in second ch from hook and in each ch across, turn—15 sc.
Row 2 and all WS Rows: Ch 1, sc in each st across, turn.
Row 3: Ch 1, *sc in first sc, [FPdc in next sc 2 rows below, sc in next 4 sc in current row, Fpdc in next sc 2 rows below, sc in next sc] twice, turn.
Row 5: Ch 1, sc in first sc, FPdc in next FPdc 2 rows below, sc in next sc in current row, skip next 5 sts, FPtr tr in third FPdc 2 rows below, going back to skipped sts, working behind the first FPtr tr, sc in next 2 sc, FPdc in second FPdc 2 rows below, sc in next sc in current row, FPdc in third FPdc 2 rows below already holding FPtr tr, sc in next 2 sc in current row, working in front of last FPtr tr, FPtr tr in second FPdc 2 rows below already holding FPtr tr, sc in next sc in current row, FPdc in next FPdc 2 rows below, sc in last sc, turn.

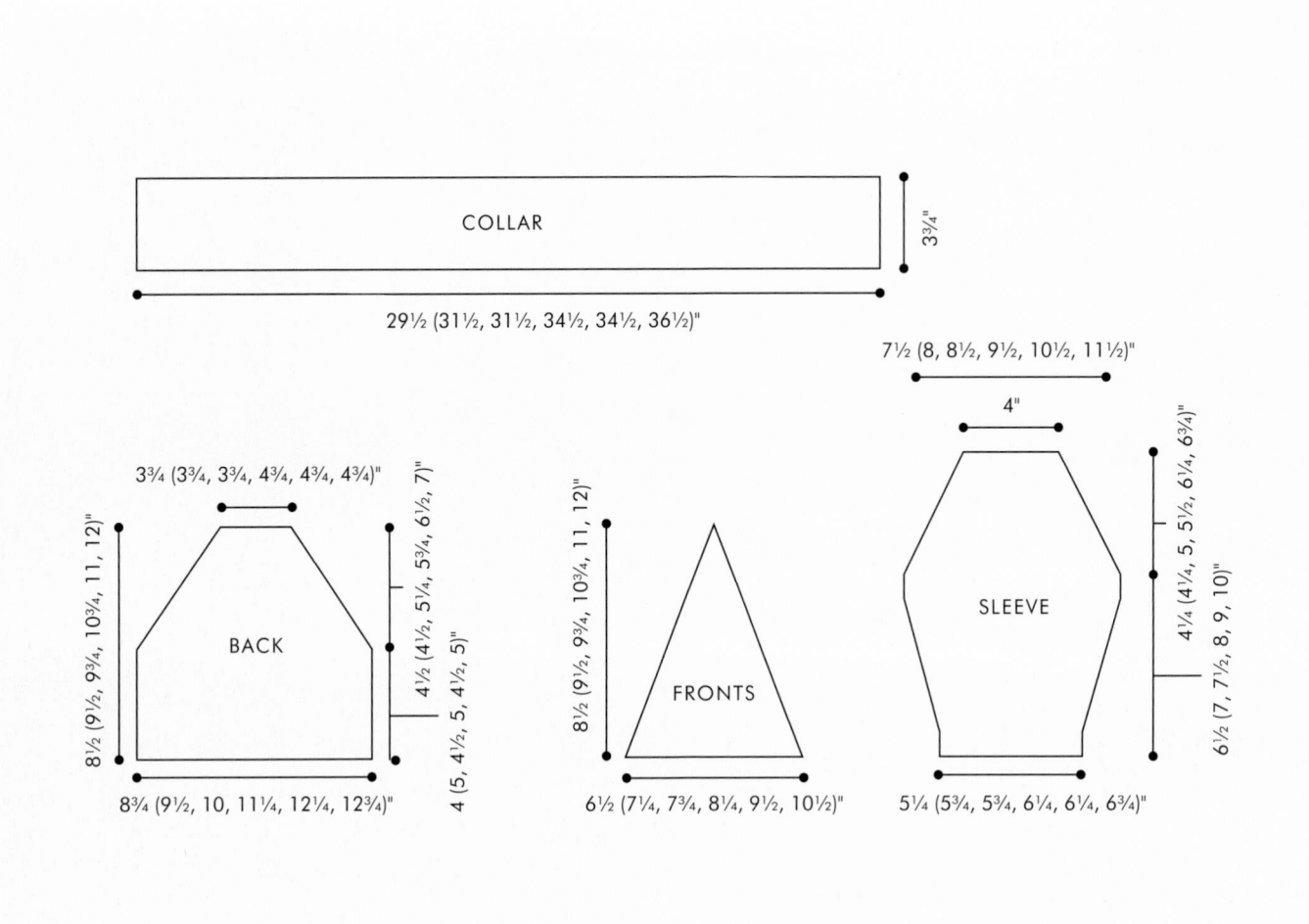

COLLAR

3¾"

29½ (31½, 31½, 34½, 34½, 36½)"

7½ (8, 8½, 9½, 10½, 11½)"

4"

3¾ (3¾, 3¾, 4¾, 4¾, 4¾)"

8½ (9½, 9¾, 10¾, 11, 12)"

BACK

4½ (4½, 5¼, 5¾, 6½, 7)"

4 (5, 4½, 5, 4½, 5)"

8¾ (9½, 10, 11¼, 12¼, 12¾)"

8½ (9½, 9¾, 10¾, 11, 12)"

FRONTS

6½ (7¼, 7¾, 8¼, 9½, 10½)"

SLEEVE

4¼ (4¼, 5, 5½, 6¼, 6¾)"

6½ (7, 7½, 8, 9, 10)"

5¼ (5¾, 5¾, 6¼, 6¼, 6¾)"

Row 7: Ch 1, sc in first sc, FPdc in next FPdc 2 rows below, sc in next sc in current row, FPdc in first FPtr tr 2 rows below, sc in next 2 sc in current row, FPdc in second FPdc 2 rows below, sc in next sc in current row, FPdc in third FPdc 2 rows below, sc in next 2 sc in current row, FPdc in second FPtr tr 2 rows below, sc in next sc in current row, FPdc in next FPdc 2 rows below, sc in last sc, turn.

Rows 9 and 11: Ch 1, sc in first sc, FPdc in next FPdc 2 rows below, sc in next sc in current row, FPdc in second FPdc 2 rows below, sc in next 2 sc in current row, FPdc in third FPdc 2 rows below, sc in next sc in current row, FPdc in fourth FPdc 2 rows below, sc in next 2 sc in current row, FPdc in fifth FPdc 2 rows below, sc in next sc in current row, FPdc in sixth FPdc 2 rows below, sc in last sc, turn.

Row 13: Ch 1, sc in first sc, FPdc in next FPdc 2 rows below, sc in next 4 sc in current row, skip 5 sts, work FPtr tr in fifth FPdc 2 rows below, going back to skipped sts, sc in next sc in current row, working in front of last FPtr tr made, work FPtr tr in second FPdc 2 rows below, sc in next 4 sc in current row, FPdc in next FPdc 2 rows below, sc in last sc, turn.

Row 15: Ch 1, sc in first sc, FPdc in next FPdc 2 rows below, sc in next 4 sc in current row, FPdc in second FPtr tr 2 rows below, sc in next sc in current row, FPdc in third FPtr tr 2 rows below, sc in next 4 sc in current row, FPdc in next FPdc 2 rows below, sc in last sc, turn.

Row 17: Ch 1, sc in first sc, FPdc in next FPdc 2 rows below, sc in next sc in current row, skip next 5 sc, FPtr tr in third FPdc 2 rows below, going back to skipped sts, working behind last FPtr tr made, sc in next 2 sc in current row, work FPdc in second FPdc 2 rows below, sc in next sc in current row, FPdc in

third FPdc 2 rows below, sc in next 2 sc in current row, working in front of last FPtr tr made, work FPtr tr in second FPdc 2 rows below, sc in next sc in current row, FPdc in next FPdc 2 rows below, sc in last sc, turn.
Repeat Rows 6-17 for Collar Pattern.

BACK

Ch 33 (35, 37, 41, 45, 47). Begin EXsc; work even for 13 (16, 15, 16, 15, 16) rows—31 (33, 35, 39, 43, 45) sts remain after first row.

SHAPE RAGLAN ARMHOLES
Next Row: Decrease 1 st each side this row, every other row 5 (4, 5, 7, 7, 8) times, then every row 3 (5, 5, 3, 5, 5) times—13 (13, 13, 17, 17, 17) sts remain. Fasten off. Piece should measure approximately 8½ (9½, 9¾, 10¾, 11, 12)".

FRONTS (make 2)

Ch 25 (27, 29, 31, 35, 39). Begin EXsc; work even for 3 rows— 23 (25, 27, 29, 33, 37) sts remain after first row.

SHAPE FRONT
Next Row: Decrease 1 st each side this row, every other row 7 (7, 9, 9, 13, 15) times, then every 4 rows 2 (3, 2, 3, 1, 1) time(s)— 3 sts remain. Work even for 1 (0, 1, 0, 1, 0) row(s).
Last Row: Ch 1, work EXsc3tog over next 3 sts. Fasten off. Piece should measure approximately 8½ (9½, 9¾, 10¾, 11, 12)".

SLEEVES

Ch 20 (22, 22, 24, 24, 26). Begin EXsc; work even for 3 rows— 18 (20, 20, 22, 22, 24) sts remain after first row.

SHAPE SLEEVE
Next Row: Increase 1 st each side this row, every 4 rows 3 (3, 3, 4, 5, 5) times, then every other row 0 (0, 1, 1, 1, 2) time(s)— 26 (28, 30, 34, 36, 40) sts. Work even until piece measures 6½ (7, 7½, 8, 9, 10)" from the beginning.

SHAPE RAGLAN ARMHOLES
Next Row: Decrease 1 st each side this row, every other row 5 (6, 7, 8, 9, 9) times, then every row 0 (0, 0, 1, 1, 3) time(s)—14 sts remain. Work even for 3 (1, 1, 0, 0, 0) row(s). Fasten off.

COLLAR

Ch 16. Begin Collar Pattern; work even until piece measures 29½ (31½, 31½, 34½, 34½, 36½)" from the beginning. Fasten off.

FINISHING

Place markers on Fronts 4½ (4½, 5¼, 5¾, 6½, 7)" down from top for armholes, measured along shaping edge. Place marker along right edge for Left Front and along left edge for Right Front. Sew raglan Sleeves to Back and Front armholes. Sew side and Sleeve seams. Sew Collar to neck edge.

Ties (make 4): Make a ch approximately 10" long. Fasten off. Make a small overhand knot at one end. Sew 1 Tie to inside right side seam, 3" up from bottom edge. Sew 1 Tie to outside left edge, 3" up from bottom edge. Sew 1 Tie to each Front at bottom edge.

Limonia Caterpillar

This cute little caterpillar is worked in vibrant, citrusy colors. The body is crafted mostly in single crochet—the easiest of stitches—and is decorated with colorful rounds of bobbles.

FINISHED MEASUREMENTS
Approximately 7" long

YARN
Berroco Comfort DK (50% super fine nylon / 50% super fine acrylic; 50 grams / 178 yards): 1 skein each #2740 Seedling (A), #2713 Dusk (B), #2734 Liquorice (C), and #2852 Cartwheel (D)

CROCHET HOOKS
One crochet hook size US F/5 (3.75 mm)
Change hook size if necessary to obtain correct gauge.

GAUGE
18 sts and 24 rows = 4" (10 cm) in Single Crochet (sc)

NOTIONS
Stuffing; tapestry needle

FACE
Using A, ch 14. Begin sc; work even until piece measures 2¼". Fasten off.

BODY
Using B, work 51 sc evenly around perimeter of Face, join with a slip st in first sc. Begin sc in rnds; work even for 3 rnds. Change to C; work even for 4 rnds.
Textured Rnd: Change to D; ch 1, sc in next 2 sc, *5 dc in next sc, sc in next 2 sc; repeat from * to last sc, 5 dc in last sc—17 5-dc shells.
Next Rnd: Change to C; ch 1, *sc in next 2 sc, skip 2 dc, sc in third dc, skip 2 dc; repeat from * to end. Work in sc for 3 rnds.
Next Rnd: Change to A; work even for 4 rnds.
Next Rnd: Change to D; repeat Textured Rnd.
Next Rnd: Change to B; ch 1, *sc in next 2 sc, skip 2 dc, sc in third dc, skip 2 dc; repeat from * to end. Work in sc for 3 rnds.
Next Rnd: Change to C; work even for 4 rnds.
Next Rnd: Change to D; repeat Textured Rnd.
Next Rnd: Change to C; ch 1, *sc in next 2 sc, skip 2 dc, sc in third dc, skip 2 dc; repeat from * to end. Work in sc for 3 rnds.
Next Rnd: Change to A; work even for 4 rnds.
Next Rnd: Change to D; repeat Textured Rnd.
Next Rnd: Change to B; ch 1, *sc in next 2 sc, skip 2 dc, sc in third dc, skip 2 dc; repeat from * to end. Work in sc for 3 rnds. Stuff Body to desired firmness.

SHAPE BODY

Decrease Rnd 1: *Sc in next 2 sc, sc2tog; repeat from * to last sc, sc in last sc—38 sts remain. Work even in sc for 1 rnd.
Decrease Rnd 2: *Sc in next 2 sc, sc2tog; repeat from * to last 2 sc, sc in last 2 sc—29 sts remain. Work even in sc for 1 rnd.
Decrease Rnd 3: *Sc in next 2 sc, sc2tog; repeat from * to last sc, sc in last sc—22 sts remain. Work even in sc for 1 rnd.
Decrease Rnd 4: *[Insert hook in next st, yo, draw up a loop] twice, yo, draw through 2 loops on hook; repeat from * to end, leaving last loop of every st on hook—11 loops on hook. Stuff remaining portion of Body. Cut yarn, leaving an 8" tail; thread tail through remaining loops on hook, pull tight, and fasten off.

ANTENNAE

Join C in top corner of head. Ch 11. Dc in fourth ch from hook and in each ch to end. Slip st in base of Antenna. Fasten off. Repeat for second Antenna at opposite corner.

LEGS

Join C on underbelly, 1 row before any dc row. Ch 7. Sc in second ch from hook and in each ch to to end. Slip st in base of Leg. Fasten off. Work 3 more Legs on same side, then 4 Legs on other side.

FINISHING

With tapestry needle and C, embroider 2 eyes with a simple straight st (see Special Techniques, page 156).

Scribble Blanket

This blanket was inspired by an art game my father taught me when I was little: Begin by filling a page with one continuous scribble, then, with a palette of four to five shades, color in the resulting shapes, making sure that no color sits next to itself. I call the result everyday abstract expressionism.

FINISHED MEASUREMENTS
39" wide x 45" long

YARN
Berroco Comfort (50% super fine nylon / 50% super fine acrylic; 100 grams / 210 yards): 3 skeins #9740 Seedling (B); 2 skeins each #9766 Sable (A), #9755 Wild Cherry (C), and #9764 Lidfors (E); 1 skein #9733 Turquoise (D)

NEEDLES
One 29" (70 cm) long circular (circ) needle size US 9 (5.5 mm)
Change needle size if necessary to obtain correct gauge.

GAUGE
18 sts and 24 rows = 4" (10 cm) in Stockinette stitch (St st)

BLANKET
Using B, CO 162 sts. Do not join. Purl 1 row.
Next Row (RS): Work 81 sts from Chart A, then 81 sts from Chart B. Work even until Charts are complete.
Next Row (RS): Work 81 sts from Chart C, then 81 sts from Chart D. Work even until Charts are complete. BO all sts using B.

FINISHING
Top and Bottom Borders: With RS facing, using B, pick up and knit 162 sts evenly along CO edge. Begin Garter st (knit every row); work even for 1½", ending with a WS row. BO all sts knitwise. Repeat for BO end.
Side Borders: With RS facing, using B, pick up and knit 202 sts along side edge of Blanket, including Top and Bottom Borders. Begin Garter st; work even for 1½", ending with a WS row. BO all sts knitwise. Repeat for opposite edge.

Block lightly (see Special Techniques, page 156).

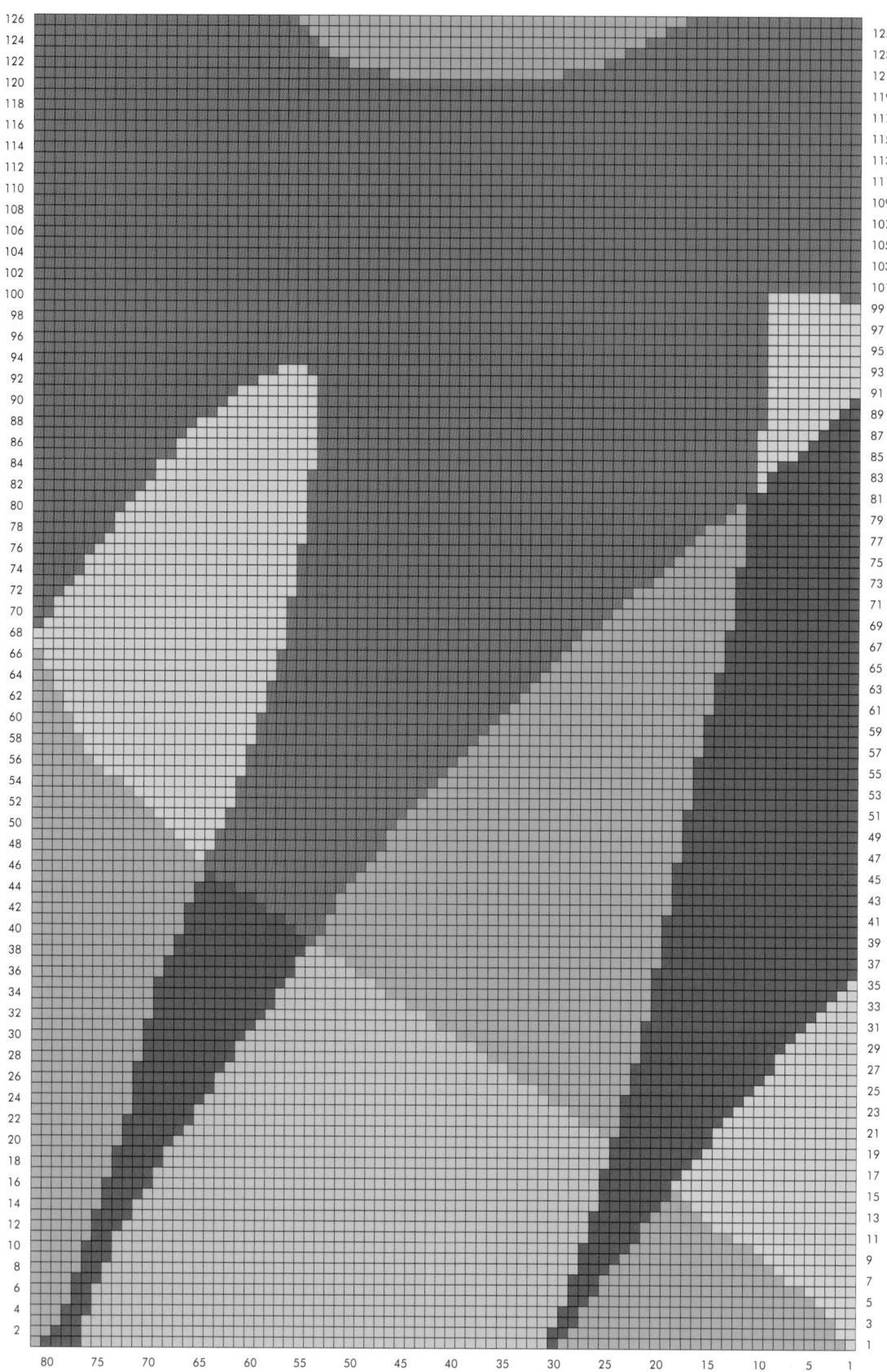

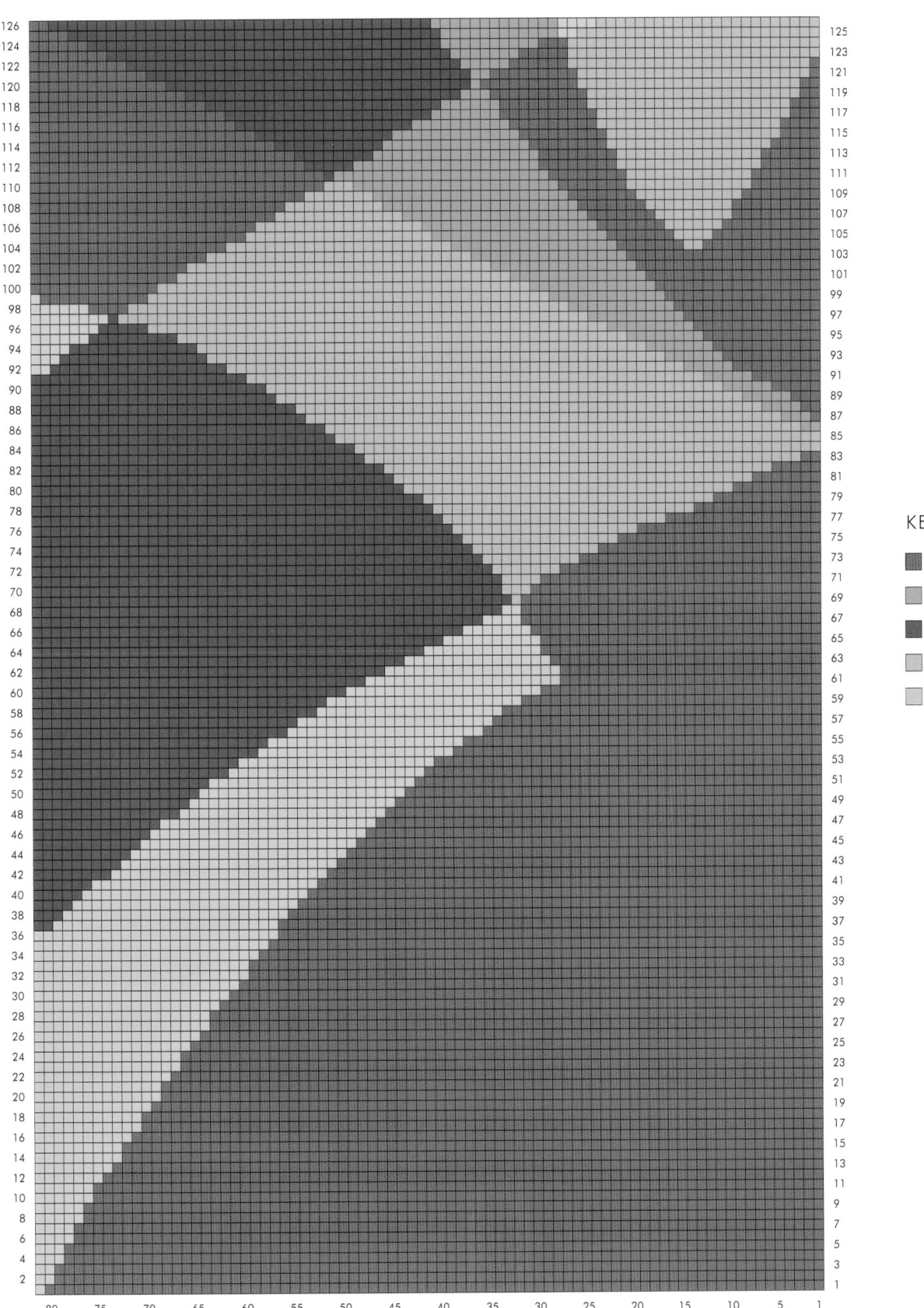

KEY

A
B
C
D
E

CHART C

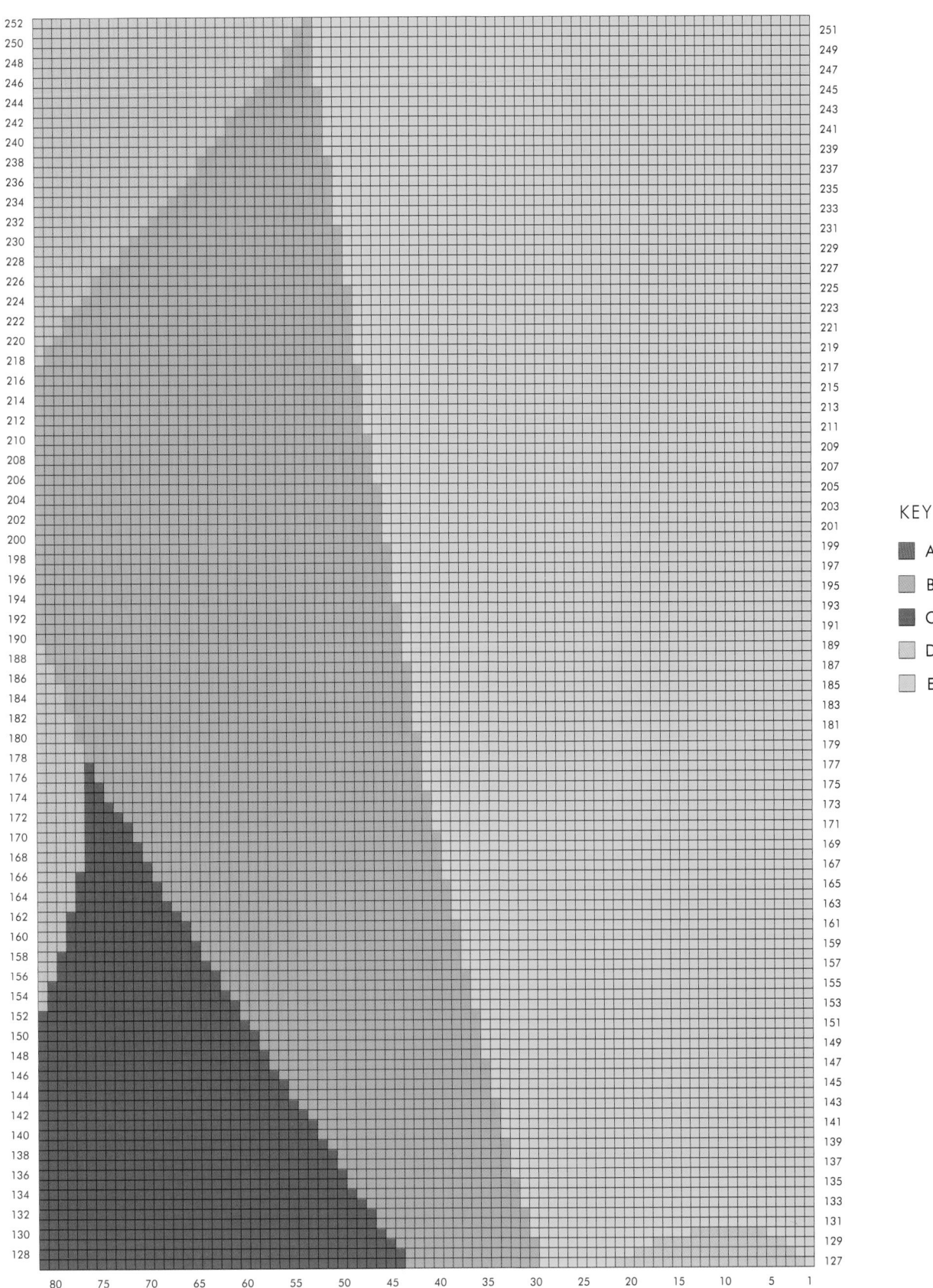

KEY

■ A
■ B
■ C
■ D
■ E

Knit

BO
Bind off

CO
Cast on

Circ
Circular

Cn
Cable needle

Dpn(s)
Double pointed needle(s)

K
Knit

K1-f/b
Knit into front loop and back loop of same st to increase 1 st.

K1-f/b/f
Knit into front loop, back loop, then front loop of same st to increase 2 sts.

K2tog
Knit 2 together

K2tog-tbl
Knit 2 together through back loops.

M1
(Make 1)
With the tip of the left-hand needle inserted from front to back, lift the strand between the two needles onto the left-hand needle; knit the strand through the back loop to increase 1 st.

M1-p
(Make 1 purlwise)
With tip of left-hand needle inserted from back to front, lift strand between 2 needles onto left-hand needle; purl strand through front loop to increase 1 stitch.

MB
Make bobble

MC
Main color

P
Purl

P2tog
Purl 2 together

P2tog-tbl
Purl 2 together through back loops.

Pm
Place marker

Rev st st
(Reverse stockinette stitch)
Purl on RS, knit on WS.

Rnd(s)
Round(s)

RS
Right side

S2kp2
Slip the next 2 sts together to the right-hand needle as if to knit 2 together, k1, pass the 2 slipped sts over.

Sk2p
Slip 1, knit 2 together, pass the slipped st over the knit st.

Sm
Slip marker

Ssk
(slip, slip, knit)
Slip 2 sts to right-hand needle one at a time as if to knit; return them back to left-hand needle one at a time in their new orientation; knit them together through the back loops.

St(s)
Stitch(es)

St st
(Stockinette stitch)
Knit on RS, purl on WS.

Tbl
Through the back loop

Wyib
With yarn in back

Wyif
With yarn in front

WS
Wrong side

Yo
Yarn over

BPdc
(Back Post double crochet)
Yo, insert hook from back to front to back around post of indicated st, yo and pull up a loop, [yo and pull through 2 loops on hook] twice.

Ch
Chain

Dc
(Double crochet)
Yarn over hook (2 loops on hook), insert hook into next st, yarn over hook and pull up a loop (3 loops on hook), [yarn over and draw through 2 loops] twice.

Dctog
(Double crochet together)
Yo, [insert hook into next dc and pull up a loop, yo and pull through 2 loops] twice, yo and pull through 3 loops on hook.

Dc4tog
(Double crochet 4 together)
Yo, [insert hook into next dc and pull up a loop, yo and pull through 2 loops] 4 times, yo and pull through all 5 loops on hook.

Dc5tog
(Double crochet 5 together)
Yo, [insert hook into next dc and pull up a loop, yo and pull through 2 loops] 5 times, yo and pull through all 6 loops on hook.

EXsc
(Extended single crochet)
Insert hook in st, yo and pull loop through st, yo, pull through 1 loop on hook, yo, pull through 2 loops on hook.

EXsc2tog
(Extended single crochet 2 together)
[Insert hook in next st, yo and pull loop through st, yo, pull through 1 loop on hook] twice, yo, pull through 3 loops on hook.

EXsc3tog
(Extended single crochet 3 together)
[Insert hook in next st, yo and pull loop through st, yo, pull through 1 loop on hook] 3 times, yo, pull through 4 loops on hook.

Fwd
Forward

FPdc
(Front Post double crochet)
Yo, insert hook from front to back to front around post of indicated st, yo and pull up a loop, [yo and pull through 2 loops on hook] twice.

FPdc decrease
(Front Post double crochet decrease)
Yo, insert hook from front to back to front around

post of indicated st, yo and pull up a loop, yo and pull through 2 loops on hook; yo, insert hook from front to back to front around post of indicated st, yo and pull up a loop, yo and draw through 2 loops on hook, yo and draw through all 3 loops on hook.

FPtr tr
(Front Post triple triple crochet)
Yo 4 times, insert hook from front to back to front around post of indicated st, yo and pull up a loop, [yo and pull through 2 loops on hook] 5 times.

Hdc
(Half double crochet)
Yarn over hook (2 loops on hook), insert hook into next st, yarn over hook and pull up a loop (3 loops on hook), yarn over hook and draw through 3 loops on hook.

Reverse sc
(Reverse single crochet)
Working from left to right, insert hook into the next st to the right, yo and pull up a loop, yo and pull through 2 loops on hook.

Rnd(s)
Round(s)

Rtn
Return

Sc
(Single crochet)
Insert hook into the next st, yo and pull up a loop, yo and pull through 2 loops on hook.

Sc2tog
(Single crochet decrease)
Pull up a loop in each of next 2 sc, yo and pull through both loops on hook.

Sc-tbl
Single crochet through back loop

Sc-tfl
Single crochet through front loop

Sk
Skip

Sp(s)
Space(s)

St(s)
Stitch(es)

Tr
(Triple crochet)
Yarn over hook twice (3 loops on hook), insert hook into next st, yo and pull up a loop (4 loops on hook), [yo and draw through 2 loops on hook] 3 times.

Yo
Yarn over

Special Techniques

KNIT

CABLE CO

Make a loop (using a slipknot) with the working yarn and place it on the left-hand needle (first st CO), knit into slip knot, draw up a loop but do not drop st from left-hand needle; place new loop on left-hand needle; *insert the tip of the right-hand needle into the space between the last 2 sts on the left-hand needle and draw up a loop; place the loop on the left-hand needle. Repeat from * for remaining sts to be CO, or for casting on at the end of a row in progress.

JOGLESS COLOR CHANGE

To minimize the jog where colors change when working stripes in the round, work one round with the new color, remove beginning of the round marker, lift the previous-color st below the next new-color st onto the left-hand needle; k2tog (lifted st of previous-color and first st of new-color), replace the marker. The beginning of the round will move 1 st to the left at each color change.

GARTER STITCH

Knit every row when working straight; knit 1 round, purl 1 round when working circular.

I-CORD

Using a double-pointed needle, cast on or pick up the required number of sts; the working yarn will be at the left-hand side of the needle. *Transfer the needle with the sts to your left hand, bring the yarn around behind the work to the right-hand side; using a second double-pointed needle, knit the sts from right to left, pulling the yarn from left to right for the first st; do not turn. Slide the sts to the opposite end of the needle; repeat from * until the I-Cord is the length desired. Note: After a few rows, the tubular shape will become apparent.

INTARSIA COLORWORK METHOD

Use a separate length of yarn for each color section; you may wind yarn onto bobbins to make color changes easier. When changing colors, bring the new yarn up and to the right of the yarn just used to twist the yarns and prevent leaving a hole; do not carry colors not in use across the back of the work.

KNITTED CO

Make a loop (using a slipknot) with the working yarn and place it on the left-hand needle (first st CO), *knit into the st on the left-hand needle, draw up a loop but do not drop st from left-hand needle; place new loop on left-hand needle; repeat from * for remaining sts to be CO, or for casting on at the end of a row in progress.

LONG-TAIL (THUMB) CO

Leaving tail with about 1" of yarn for each st to be cast on, make a slipknot in the yarn and place it on the right-hand needle, with the tail to the front and the working end to the back. Insert the thumb and forefinger of your left hand between the strands of yarn so that the working end is around your forefinger, and the tail end is around your thumb "slingshot" fashion; *insert the tip of the right-hand needle into the front loop on the thumb, hook the strand of yarn coming from the forefinger from back to front, and draw it through the loop on your thumb; remove your thumb from the loop and pull on the working yarn to tighten the new st on the right-hand needle; return your thumb and forefinger to their original positions, and repeat from * for remaining sts to be CO.

READING CHARTS

Unless otherwise specified in the instructions, when working straight, charts are read from right to left for RS rows, from left to right for WS rows. Row numbers are written at the beginning of each row. Numbers on the right indicate RS rows; numbers on the left indicate WS rows. When working circular, all rounds are read from right to left.

REVERSE STOCKINETTE STITCH (REV ST ST)

Purl on RS rows, knit on WS rows when working straight; purl every round when working circular.

RIBBING

Although rib stitch patterns use different numbers of sts, all are worked in the same way, whether straight or circular. The instructions will specify how many sts to knit or purl; the example below uses k1, p1.

Row/Rnd 1: *K1, p1; repeat from * across (end k1 if an odd number of sts).

Row/Rnd 2: Knit the knit sts and purl the purl sts as they face you.

Repeat Row/Rnd 2 for rib st.

STOCKINETTE STITCH (ST ST)

Knit on RS rows, purl on WS rows when working straight; knit every round when working circular.

STRANDED (FAIR ISLE) COLORWORK METHOD

When more than one color is used per row, carry color(s) not in use loosely across the WS of work. Be sure to secure all colors at beginning and end of rows to prevent holes.

THREE-NEEDLE BO

Place the sts to be joined onto two same-size needles; hold the pieces to be joined with RSs facing each other and the needles parallel, both pointing to the right. Holding both needles in your left hand, using working yarn and a third needle same size or one size larger, insert third needle into first st on front needle, then into first st on back needle; knit these two sts together; *knit next st from each needle together (two sts on right-hand needle); pass first st over second st to BO one st. Repeat from * until one st remains on third needle; cut yarn and fasten off.

YARNOVER (YO) OTHER THAN BEGINNING OF ROW

Bring yarn forward (to the purl position), then place it in position to work the next st. If next st is to be knit, bring yarn over the needle and knit; if next st is to be purled, bring yarn over the needle and then forward again to the purl position and purl. Work the yarnover in pattern on the next row unless instructed otherwise.

CROCHET

CROCHET CHAIN

Make a slipknot and place it on crochet hook. Holding tail end of yarn in left hand, *take hook under ball end of yarn from front to back; draw yarn on hook back through previous st on hook to form new st. Repeat from * to desired number of sts or length of chain.

REVERSE SINGLE CROCHET

Work from left to right for right-handers, or from right to left for left-handers. *Insert hook into previous single crochet, yo hook, pull through to RS—2 loops on hook. Yo hook, draw through both loops—1 loop on hook. Repeat from * to end. Fasten off.

SLIDING LOOP

Wrap yarn clockwise over left hand one or two fingers, two times to form a ring. Holding yarn tail away to the left, insert hook into ring and pull the working yarn through the ring. Work in ring as directed. When last st is worked, pull the tail lightly to tighten the ring.

EMBROIDERY

BACKSTITCH

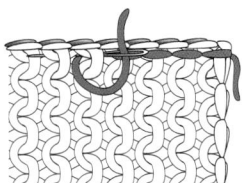

Bring tapestry needle up from WS to RS through first hole, then take needle back to WS through second hole. Bring yarn back to RS through third hole, then back to WS through second hole. Continue in this manner, working from WS to RS in empty hole beyond last hole worked, then going backwards one hole to go from RS to WS.

CHAIN STITCH

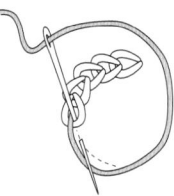

Repeat the stitch as shown above to create a curved or straight line of Chain Stitches.

CROSS STITCH

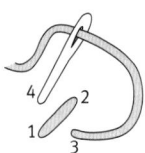

Repeat the stitch as shown above to create a line of Cross Stitches.

FRENCH KNOT

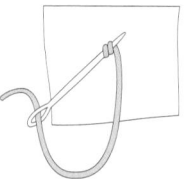

Thread a tapestry needle and bring the needle up from the WS. Wrap the yarn 2 or 3 times tightly around the needle tip. Hold the wrapped yarn in place and bring the needle to the WS, about ⅛" from where it came up. Pull the rest of the working yarn through the knot.

RUNNING STITCH/STRAIGHT STITCH

Running Stitch and Straight Stitch are worked the same, (the former along curved lines, and the latter along straight lines).

SATIN STITCH

Cover an area with closely spaced straight stitches as follows: Bring threaded needle from WS to RS of fabric at one edge of area to be covered. *At opposite edge of area, bring needle from RS to WS and back to RS, catching smallest possible bit of background fabric. Repeat from *, carefully tensioning the stitches so work lies flat without puckering.

BLOCKING

To flatten seams or neaten the overall look of a finished piece, dampen the piece slightly with a spray bottle or damp cloth, finger press affected areas and lay flat to dry.

When a more serious blocking is needed, for color work or stretching a piece to full size, wet completely, pin to a flat surface and let dry.

Steam or heat is not recommended.

HISTORY OF BERROCO

When Warren Wheelock's great-great-great-grandfather opened the first of the Wheelock Mills in rural Massachusetts in 1810, he began a dynamic enterprise that has endured over six generations. Beginning as Stanley Woolen Mills, the firm survived two depressions, weathering changing times and evolving demands in the world of textiles. In 1968, the Wheelock family formed a new hand-knitting subsidiary. This new firm grew to become one of the largest importers and wholesalers of hand-knitting yarns and patterns to independent yarn shops in the United States and Canada. Operating on the site of one of the Wheelock family's original woolen mills, Berroco, Inc., continues the family tradition of changing with the needs of the times to provide top-quality products.

THE YARNS

All of the items in *Comfort Knitting & Crochet: Babies & Toddlers* were made with Berroco Comfort or Berroco Vintage. Both are available in worsted, DK, and chunky weights in a multitude of shades. To view Comfort or Vintage shade cards, find a store, or for other information about the yarns, visit www.berroco.com or email info@berroco.com.

DESIGN CREDITS

The Berroco design team is indeed a team. It's difficult to assign just one designer's name to most of the projects in this book because of how we work together. Quite often several people have had a hand in any one design by the time it's finished, and we frequently make decisions together. While I did most of the sketching of the original ideas, Amanda Keep sketched as well. Brenda York made many of our ideas come to fruition, adding details and helping to perfect them along the way. Following are design credits for designs worked on primarily by individuals:

Norah Gaughan: Cleire Cardigan, Compass Cap, Hike Hat, Moderne Blanket, Orangelo Bib, Paddington Coat, Rag Rug Blanket, Solaria Blanket

Amanda Keep: Abigail Bolero, Battenberg Blanket, Bobbled Blanket, Camellia Blanket, Havilland Blanket, Limoges Blanket, Limonia Caterpillar, Pomelo Slice, Rivulet Blanket, "Smocked" Cardigan, Sunday Best Dress, Tuxedo Romper

Brenda York: "Aran" Blanket, Bertie Bird, Butterfly Blanket, Citron Blanket, Darla Blanket, High Fidoodlity Blanket, Snowflake Blanket

ACKNOWLEDGMENTS

This book would not have been possible without the contributions of Brenda York, who swatched and perfected many of the items in the book. Likewise, many thanks to Donna Yacino, who organized the making of the projects and kept track of what went where (which was not a small task). Amanda Keep's strong independent work skills helped keep us on schedule, and she came through in a pinch with a beautiful grouping of teacup-inspired pieces. Thanks to the many knitters and crocheters without whom the projects in this book would not have come to fruition. Many, many thanks to Barbara Khouri for her pattern-writing skills, persistence, patience, and friendship, all of which were greatly appreciated. Thanks also to Russ Sherwin, and his friends Jody Rhoads, Bobby Richard, and Jeanetta Miller, for letting us use their photo from 1942 on page 6.

Lastly, thanks to the endless patience of my husband, John Ranta, whose children have recently brought two grandbabies into my life—which I couldn't be happier about.

WARDROBE, TOYS, AND DECOR PROVIDED BY:

Serena & Lily
www.serenaandlily.com

Rikshaw Design
www.rikshawdesign.com

Peace Industry
www.peaceindustry.com

Lola Home Design by Lois Vinsel
www.lolahome.com

Atomic Garden
www.atomicgardenoakland.com

Peek Kids
www.peekkids.com